APPLIQUE STITCHERY

Plate 1. **Rare Seeds.** 30 by 54 inches. Couched stems and satin-stitch seeds form a linear pattern on blue wool.

APPLIQUE STITCHERY

Jean Ray Laury

Plate 2. Apple.

REINHOLD BOOK CORPORATION

NEW YORK AMSTERDAM LONDON

All color and black-and-white photography by Gayle Smalley, with the
exception of Plate 9, Courtesy of the *Fresno Bee,* photograph by
Carl Crawford; and Plates 19 and 32, photographs by George McLean.
All drawings and examples of stitchery are the work of the author.

ABOUT THIS BOOK

Nearly ten years ago I first discovered stitchery. That discovery led to hours of absorbing work, to the writing of this book, to quantities of unwashed dishes, and to my present enthusiasm for stitchery.

It is only fair to warn the newcomer to stitchery that she may find it addicting. There never seems to be a place to stop — no chapter ends at which to quit for the night. Finding time to devote to stitchery is rarely a problem. The problem comes only in finding time to devote to the less exciting shopping and cleaning tasks of day-to-day living.

Your home can readily become a studio for stitchery. The needs are simple, the tools few. Such a studio is usually characterized by a beautiful array of fabric trimmings and a large basket of unironed clothes. Children thrive in such an environment, guests enjoy it, and all accept your wielding a needle as you visit.

My own work in stitchery has grown in part from an enjoyment of nature. For this I thank my mother, who always found the first pussy willows of spring or the milkweed pods of fall to be as important as homemade jam or polished floors.

It is with some chagrin that I thank my husband Frank for plucking out the most absurd phrases and lines from my manuscript before anyone else saw them; and I happily thank him for maintaining (almost always) a remarkable sense of humor.

For the superb photographs I am indebted to Gayle Smalley, who sandwiched between her teaching and graduate study the meticulous photographic work.

I am grateful to my children, Tom and Liz. Their constant interruptions forced me to organize my time and to do my writing during their school hours. Their unsolicited evaluations of my work were sometimes dismaying, always honest, and surprisingly insightful.

I specially thank Professor Matt Kahn of Stanford University for his inspired teaching, Dr. June King McFee for her encouragement, and Bob Beeching for his enthusiastic response to this whole project. Finally I thank my friends Ruth Law, Joyce Aiken, and Stan Bitters, whose blunt and constant questions regarding the progress of this book kept me prodded into action.

CONTENTS

COLOR PLATES

Plate 3. Quilt block. The simplest appliqué and embroidery stitches are used in this design, which is one of a series for a cotton quilt.

ABOUT STITCHERY

Appliqué stitchery can be profound, decorative, moving, humorous, or loving. It is a charming, personal, and vital art form, using the humble materials of every day to offer unpretentious works of real value and deep meaning.

Just what is appliqué stitchery? Appliqué is the surface attachment of one fabric to another piece of fabric by any of various means — usually by sewing. It is similar to the collage technique used with paper in that it suggests overlapping of layers. Stitchery is a loose and general term for work done with a needle or by stitching. It is somewhat all-inclusive, involving any work with threads, floss, yarns, or cord. Objects held to fabric with stitches could also fall into this category as do the various kinds of embroidery.

Stitchery means much the same as needlework, but avoids the connotation of stamped patterns, directions, and limitations. It exchanges the sterility and triteness of most pattern work for a more individual and inventive use of the same materials and tools. Stitchery is freer and less confining. All materials and methods, either hand or machine sewn, are included.

Appliqué stitchery, then, refers to a creative approach in the use of fabrics applied to other fabrics by various means of sewing and embroidery. This book is intended to aid or guide anyone interested in the general area of stitchery, with an emphasis on the inventive and personal use of appliqué and embroidery.

The renewed interest in stitchery brings back to us some of the personal warmth so much needed in our homes. In the hand-sewn stitches, in the cut shapes, we feel the presence of the artists who produce them, whether they are early American or contemporary. Our homes today are filled largely with manufactured items. They come to us crated, "untouched by human hands." We buy articles mummified in Mylar, bound in protective polyethylene and marked "sterile." These mass-produced articles, each identical to the others of its kind, are impersonal. In many respects, they tend to make our homes identical. These manufactured items satisfy many needs: we want them, use them, and need them. But it is important to recognize what they do for us and to understand what they cannot do. We must see which needs they fill and which needs they do not satisfy.

As manufactured items increasingly replace handmade articles we lose evidence of some human involvement in our everyday environment. With mass production there is an obvious loss of consideration for the individual. In your grandmother's time, for example, a carved wooden spoon was made to fit the hand of the woman who used it. Today, the form of your stainless steel spoon is determined in part by the flat sheet out of which the machine has cut it. The product is consequently less personal. Undoubtedly, a cake mixed with one will taste the same as the cake mixed with the other, but the experience of mixing the cake is different.

When nights turn chilly and you need an extra cover, a machine-made blanket will stop your shivers, but a handmade quilt satisfies something far beyond the physical need for warmth. The evident devotion displayed in these everyday articles gives them an added significance. It produces a tie, a thread of communication, between the person who makes them and the person using them. If you prefer a handmade object, you have something that is functional and in addition a work that served as an expressive channel for the craftsman or artist. It is through these expressions that we see another person's outlook or view. This interpretation or response is essential to any art form. Appliqué stitchery is just one of many media through which personal involvement is possible. In the cut shapes and the stitches, simple, humble, and happy ideas are so often expressed.

Art has less to do with the material used than with the perceptive and expressive abilities of the individual. Any difference between the "fine" and the "decorative" arts is not a matter of material, but rather what the artist brings to the material. Any media may successfully be used at any level for any purpose. Just as artists' oils can become highly decorative, stitchery too can be adapted to the artist's individual needs.

It is important to work with a medium over which you have control. Sometimes this involves trying many different media, and fabric could happily be one of those. Because we are all accustomed to handling fabric everyday, it may be easier to work with. There is less resistance to the material itself, as it is part of our everyday activities. Few of us have never used a needle and thread.

Stitchery is for everyone who wishes to try it, regardless of age or experience. If you have needle and thread, bits and scraps of fabrics, and scissors that will actually cut, you possess the basic tools and materials. There must further be a real desire to do the work; from that desire patience and skill will grow. Finally, to give the work meaning, there must be some object or purpose to the work. Perhaps you wish to do some stitchery for your home — a panel for a hallway, a pillow for a sunny window seat, a quilt of favorite play things for a child, a decoration for a holiday or special occasion, or a surprise for a friend. Or the stitchery may be a vehicle for expression and take form because of a strong response to something. You may wish to remember the glowing colors of autumn foliage, a blossoming cactus or crocus, a pet, the house you lived in as a child, an old car you once owned, a mountain trip, or ripe persimmons on a tree. Even colors formed into patterns, abstract shapes, or textural arrangements may offer a wonderful beginning.

Appliqué lends itself to a great variety of expression. Appliquéd lines can be graceful and curved or geometric and rigid. They can be as simple or complex as one's ideas and skills allow. Skills grow as ideas grow, and once you have determined what it is you wish to do, the means of doing it are easily found.

Anyone who can sew a simple in-and-out stitch has the basic skill for hand appliqué. This single running stitch is all one needs to begin. My own work in appliqué was begun with no more knowledge of stitching than that running stitch, and it was sufficient for many works. Later, other stitches were added as needed. If you can be inventive or playful with basic stitches, you will soon discover new stitches. There is no need to be concerned with all the stitches and their variations in the beginning. It is the idea that is essential and the personal involvement that gives real value. Techniques will come as you progress.

There are only two basic appliqué stitches particularly important to the beginner: running stitch and blind stitch. For embroidery, which may be used to embellish or emphasize aspects of your appliqué, that same basic running stitch is still the most versatile. Beyond that, two or three others will satisfy most needs. What is essential is an approach which allows flexible use of these few. These stitches will all be covered in Chapter 4. For machine appliqué the process simply involves using a machine that has a zigzag stitch. Specific directions for this kind of work are also given and discussed in Chapter 4.

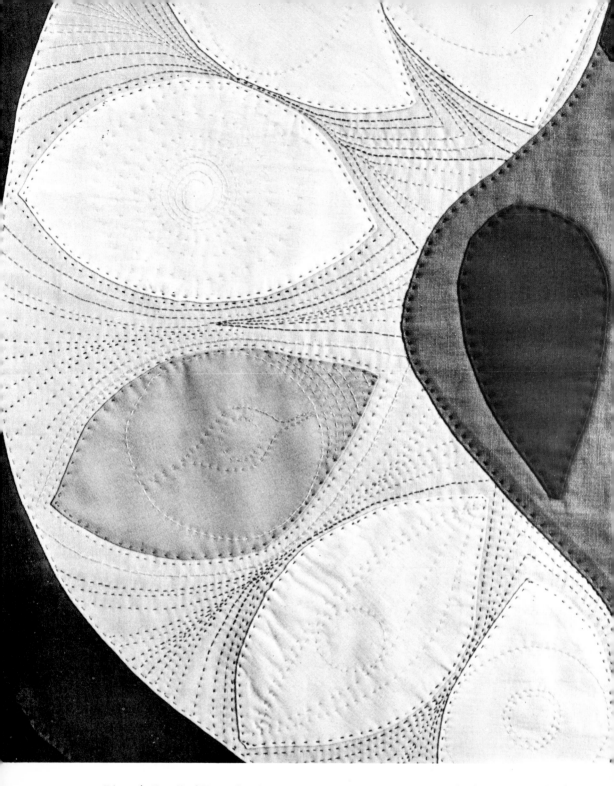

Plate 4. Detail of **Eve's Apple.** The simple running stitch is used for both the appliqué and embroidery in this panel of cotton percale.

Once ideas have sprouted and materials have been selected, many potential stitchers hesitate. Perhaps they are afraid to draw, or they are hesitant to cut into the fabric. Many are reluctant to work without a pattern or a guide, or they fear making a mistake. If you are one of these, this book is designed to help you find ways of working that will encourage you and help you to overcome these fears. One day you will find that you are selecting colors and cutting designs with ease, just as our great-grandmothers did, as folk artists have done for centuries, and as our own children do. They do not rely on the designs and directions of others — they create their own. You can do the same.

To give real value to stitchery, it must be your own. When you work out your ideas, select the colors you most enjoy, and find the most suitable stitches, the work becomes entirely yours. Now you begin to know the real pleasure of this work. You will have created something of value to yourself as well as to others.

Stitchery is one of our few surviving folk arts. As such, it is more than mere decoration or a charming pastime. The ideas come from the concerns of everyday life, the materials are humble. This very unpretentious basis allows for a reflection of those things nearest to one's heart; it allows us a glimpse into the nature of the person who created the work. Early American quilts and coverlets reflect events of interest to the pioneer woman. The subject matter came from all those things she worked with, people she loved, the countryside she saw, or the objects of her dreams. The limited materials often necessitated invention in method and design. The craftsmanship of the work indicates to us how much she cared. Today, with the range of fibers, colors, and weaves available to us, there are unlimited possibilities. If we can just retain the simplicity, honesty, and direct freshness found in these early American examples, we will have achieved much of what endures in all art.

While appliqué stitchery has given us many treasures of rich personal expression, it is by no means limited to use in the home. Many professional artists and designers have found in stitchery a wonderfully flexible decorative medium with a great range of architectural applications. Panels, stitchery tapestries, and wall hangings enrich the interiors of offices, lobbies, churches, restaurants, and public buildings.

Children, too, respond enthusiastically to the colors as well as the "cut out" technique. For them, it is similar to working in cut papers, but it offers the added tactile pleasure of textures and the awareness of greater permanence.

It is the purpose of this book to suggest some of the many directions which appliqué stitchery may take. For the designer there is the possibility of using stitchery in architectural decoration. For the homemaker there is the experience and pleasure of stitchery that may be used in her home. Mothers and group leaders will find suggestions for ways in which children can participate in stitchery projects. And for teachers, this is an art form appropriate at all levels since the needs for work space, time and materials are so flexible that no one need be deprived of its pleasures. Finally, for any individual, here is a personal approach to a totally absorbing medium, presented with the hope that each will find in stitchery the joy of challenge and satisfaction.

It is not possible to tell someone else how to work, or exactly what to do. But it is possible to describe those things which have been important to me, and perhaps they will serve to guide you. Solutions to the difficulties encountered through experience can be passed along to help you avoid similar problems.

There are no rules in stitchery — no single "right" way of working. Some procedures may work best under certain circumstances, but not in others. No two projects are exactly alike, and therefore the procedure will vary. A stitch which seems right in one case may seem inappropriate for another. Hand sewing and machine sewing are both excellent ways of working, but at times one will be clearly more appropriate and preferable to the other. The use of each will be discussed in terms of the project, the fabrics and the size.

The information presented here is basic in nature: where to begin, how to approach the work, what things to consider. It will serve as a guide in determining a sense of direction, or purpose. Furthermore, it will offer practical and specific suggestions on accomplishing this purpose. Here, then, is my effort to assist you in the discovery of that direction, and, once found, to help you enjoy all the pleasures of appliqué stitchery.

1

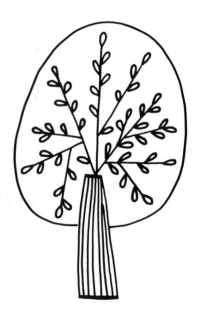

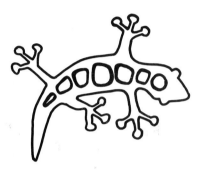

SOURCES OF IDEAS

WHERE TO LOOK FOR IDEAS

Beetles, bottles, pebbles, daisies, or trees all offer ideas for stitchery. List the things you enjoy, the objects that interest or attract you, and you have endless possibilities; the sun, the moon, apples, tigers, windows, or children. A favorite color will suggest directions. Yellows bring to mind sunshine, buttercups, autumn leaves, lemons. We associate many objects with specific colors, and each color brings with it feelings of freshness, excitement, gaiety, or calm.

Ideas may be found in familiar everyday surroundings; they are simply there waiting to be discovered. Inspiration may come from works done in the past, encouragement may come from friends or family, but ideas must come from your own experiences and responses.

SELECTING AN IDEA

Turn first to your own surroundings. As a homemaker, I spend part of each day in the kitchen, part in the garden, some with books, and much of it with children. Each offers a world of inspiration.

Teachers or mothers of small children find that the things which fill a child's day, as well as his imagination, are a constant source of delight and ideas — blocks, tricycles, ice cream cones, and dragons. For a child the fork and spoon take on great importance, and each new object is a thing of wonder. It is these everyday objects — cup, pitcher, candle, or toothbrush — which can serve as beginnings for stitchery. Figures 1 and 2 depict a few of these objects which lend themselves to stitchery.

Figure 1. Dolls, buggies, blocks, and bears all offer ideas which can be adapted to stitchery.

Figure 2. Children are delighted by everyday objects which may seem hum-drum and ordinary to adults.

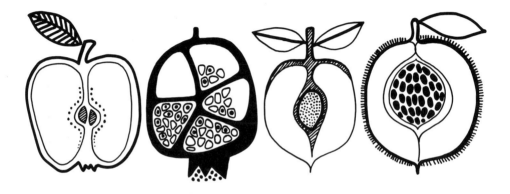

Figure 3. As you cut into a piece of fruit, take time to enjoy the beautiful patterns revealed in the cross-sections.

What can you find in your kitchen? When you pare an apple, cut a cross section and look at it. Figure 3 came from such cross sections. Slice through an artichoke and one of nature's less familiar wonders awaits you. Foliage cuttings in bottles, or jars of canned fruit (Figures 4 and 5), the mint sprig and ice cubes in a cold drink, all suggest suitable subjects. The things you like and enjoy in other ways will also appeal to you as subjects for stitchery.

If you walk or ride each day as you go to work or school, an entire new series of subjects appears: buildings, trees in parks, bus stops, benches, cars, signs and signals. Children's games on sidewalks form intriguing patterns, as do window boxes, railings or fences, bicycles lined up in their stands, and delivery cars. Take another look at the things you pass each day and you will find a world unnoticed.

Figure 4. Look all around you for ideas. Foliage cuttings in bottles on your windowsill may offer a beginning.

Figure 5. Canned fruits, jellies, and jams provide pattern and color for stitchery designs.

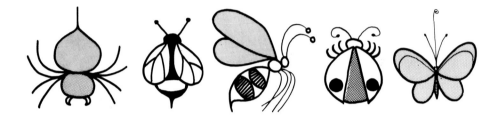

Figure 6. A garden is an unlimited source of inspiration. Before you brush away the lady bugs or squash the spider, stop to look at them and enjoy their unique forms.

Figure 7. A mouse's-eye view of weeds or grass shows delicate patterns of lines and seeds.

The garden is unlimited. Take time to pick up a beetle, a moth, or a caterpillar and examine it (Figure 6). Pull the weeds, but before tossing them on the weed pile, look at them. Take the flowers apart. Each petal is an arrangement of shapes, lines, and colors. Stop to see your flower bed in terms of patterns — the spots of color, the daisies in prim rows, the carpeting of moss roses, or the sturdy geraniums.

Plants and flowers have always been a delightful and endless source of design. You need only stop and look — and in looking, put yourself in another position. See Figures 7 and 8. When you are stretched out on the ground, the flower bed assumes a new importance. Blossoms tower overhead. Look at the butterfly with a bird's-eye view, and at the flower with

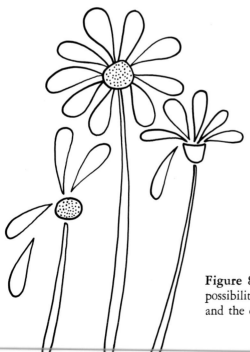

Figure 8. All things that grow in your yard are possibilities for stitchery. Even the common daisy and the dandelion have charm.

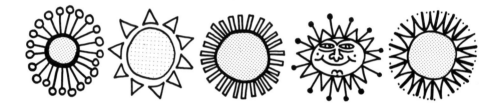

Figure 9. Each idea leads to another. In one drawing of a subject you will find suggestions for variations.

a bee's-eye view. You can be visually stimulated by all the things surrounding you, but you must open your eyes and let all the colors and patterns pour in. The tiniest amount of curiosity will open the way to surprises. Remember, too, that once you have tried an idea you have not exhausted it as a source, you have only begun to explore its possibilities. It is when you work that ideas grow fastest. As you design a sun-burst, more possibilities for the design emerge, and variations grow out of designs already conceived. Figure 9 suggests just a few variations on the sun.

My own first attempt in stitchery was to sew for my son, then four years old, a quilt full of all those things he played with: toothpaste, electric cords, salt and pepper shakers, ice cream cones, measuring spoons, pans, and (occasionally) toys. Each of these objects is simple and ordinary. Together, they form a complex and lively collection (Figure 10).

Figure 10. All the toys and tools which interested my son were appliquéd onto this quilt. While the total looks complex, each block is a simple design and was worked separately.

INVOLVEMENT WITH THE IDEA

Once you have determined the kinds of ideas that interest you, your involvement has begun. You respond to some things; they appeal to you. The stronger your feelings about the idea, the more exciting and more effortless the work becomes. Sometimes the nature of a project suggests appropriate subject material. A child's quilt, of course, opens up the possibility of using play things for appliqué designs. A pillow for a specific person may reflect a particular interest of that person — a musical instrument, sail boat, tennis racket, flower garden, or the mountains. In developing a plan, or idea, you become involved in personal interests. Your involvement occurs in three ways; through idea, attitude, and act.

THE IDEA

The subject, or idea, may be as easily identified as a tree, a flower, or a bird. Or it may be more abstract, as "growth" or "flight." Whatever direction it takes, it begins with the thought. The idea, in this sense, is what you think. It is an intellectual involvement in your work. It is an image you recall, an object you enjoy, a thought upon which other ideas build.

THE ATTITUDE

This involves how you feel about the subject, the attitudes and feelings that it evokes and your responses and impressions. If, for example, your subject is simply "tree," then your attitude determines the nature of that tree. It may be an orderly arrangement of leaves balanced on a sturdy solid trunk. Or the tree may be a maternal, all-encompassing form nurturing birds, bees, flowers, and fruits. Trees may be delicate and willowy or they may be choking and oppressive. Whatever the subject, you have feelings regarding it. This constitutes the emotional involvement in the work. See Figure 11.

THE ACT

The act of doing the work involves the craftsmanship, the skill and the techniques. It encompasses the choice of fabrics, methods, the tools — and it determines the final form. This is the physical involvement. The method is significant, but without a valid involvement with attitude and act, it becomes mere technique.

The idea or intellectual content will give a work its validity; the attitude or emotional content gives it its strength; the act or physical involvement gives it its form. This is true in all media. The specific material you select is not its most significant aspect.

The degree to which these three have been satisfactorily and successfully combined will determine how personal, individual, and significant
the work is. These involvements are not necessarily conscious ones.
Certainly in children's art and in folk art we find strong expressive and
artistic work in which the three combine into a harmonious and satisfying total. The overemphasis on a single area results in a lack of unity or
an incompleteness. Perhaps the most obvious example is that of "number
paintings" or needlework kits. In these, one's involvement is a physical
one — that of producing. The very things which could give painting a
meaning and importance (the idea, and one's feelings about it) are
eliminated. Perhaps it has the value, as some claim, of being therapeutic.
If so, fine — but therapy is not our concern in stitchery as an art form.

The therapeutic value is minimal, it seems to me, if one's involvement
is not personal. Patients cannot help but be insulted with some of the
insipid and meaningless ideas they routinely execute in order to develop
dexterity or skill; they are being deprived of the real pleasures of the
work. The same skills can as readily develop with ideas which are com-
prehensively of more personal value.

Figure 11. A tree can take many different forms. Use the forms which best describe the
kind of tree you have in mind, whether sturdy, willowy, fragile, covered with flowers, or
filled with tree-houses.

The development of skills or craftsmanship is, of course, also important. Your skill will improve as you continue to sew, and these skills will develop in accordance with your need. If you have really determined what you want to do, figuring out *how* is less difficult. As your interest in the work increases, the care with which you work increases. As you value your ideas and your feelings, your craftsmanship improves. Sloppy results are usually related to a sloppy or haphazard approach. Your craftsmanship indicates the value you place on what you do.

When children become excited about stitchery, they do not need to be shown the various stitches. They will invent their own through need. And the freshness which results cannot be achieved through the rigid teaching of processes.

To be significant, work must be personally meaningful. Speak only for yourself. You need not try to comment on the world, or on all mankind. Try, rather, to make a simple and honest statement about a single idea with which you are familiar. If you succeed in this, your specific comment is far more likely to contain a general element of truth.

As I am neither a deep thinker nor a profound one, I make no attempt to be profound in my work. I can offer only a personal response, and if that response arrives at something basic, it will evoke a response in someone else.

There are two essentials to be learned in approaching stitchery as an art form. The first is to learn to see. The second is to learn to care. Learning to see requires looking with expectancy. Nothing is insignificant. Look again at the familiar things and try to see them with a new perspective, a new point of view. Visualize the flower being six feet across and you see details never before noticed. Visualize your neighborhood from above, and the yards, rooftops, and gardens form a pattern you otherwise do not see. Learning to care means valuing your ideas, your feelings and your time. When you value these, you will find them worth the time and the effort required in true craftsmanship. If you care enough, you can learn any techniques. Mastering the skills is a matter only of determined patience and effort. If you know what you want to do, figuring out how will not be a problem.

AN APPROACH TO ORIGINALITY

No one needs to make a conscious effort to be original; such an attempt at originality can be stifling. Uniqueness is largely a matter of honesty, directness, or clarity. What seems to one person to be an obvious simple observation will, to another, seem unique and original. We place too much emphasis on being original. When a conscious effort is made at originality it becomes merely "different" and possibly, freakish. If you design simply and directly, considering what is important to you personally, freshness and originality will emerge naturally in your work.

Few ideas are really original. Our designs result in part from all we have observed in nature, from pictures, photographs, other's ideas, and other's interpretations. We reassemble these to meet our own requirements, to satisfy our own standards. We juggle the parts until they express what we wish to say.

Figure 12. Two drawings by a seven-year-old suggest the special appeal that animals have for all children.

Plate 5. Butterfly.

A stitchery class of mine was once asked to cut fruits and vegetables in half so that they could develop designs and patterns from these cross-sections. One class member noticed that she was one of three who had selected an apple and commented that they were all going to end up with the same thing. It was particularly interesting to see the three works when completed. They were entirely different in concept, and not at all similar in color or form. One, strong in color and bold in form, was a large red-skinned apple which enclosed a sturdy core of seeds. It was simple, and direct. The apple to this person was a nearly solid ball. A second was essentially the design of the seeds, and the surrounding parts, with the contour of the apple relatively unimportant. It seemed the apple was a pulpiness meant only to be a seed container. The third was light and pale in color, with fine lines and delicate stem. Each had worked from an apple section almost identical to the others. Each felt that she had made a "true" copy. Actually, each had interpreted the apple's form in a different way, selecting the parts to be emphasized, and the parts to be eliminated.

It seems, therefore, we need not be concerned about "copying" from nature. It is the source for all natural form, and whatever we do will be an interpretation. We extract those portions that have significance to us. We draw upon these sources, and our designs (while not completely "original") are certainly personal interpretations. Each person's designs will be unique.

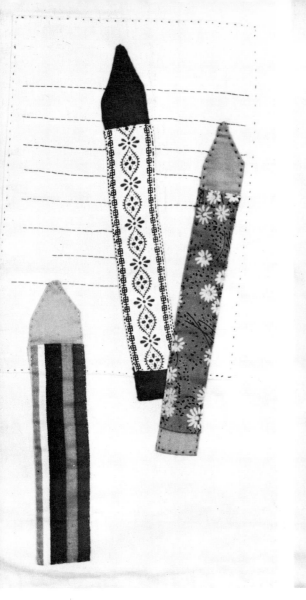

Plate 6. Crayons.

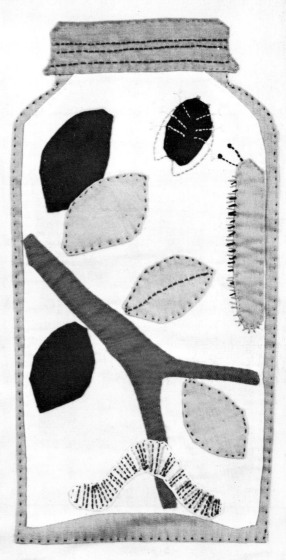

Plate 7. Insect Jar.

Plates 5, 6, 7, and 8 show block designs for a child's quilt. Crayons and caterpillars, butter-flies and bugs, all the everyday wonders become part of a child's quilt.

OTHER SOURCES OF IDEAS

Clippings from magazines, photographs, and drawings can be helpful in providing outside sources — that is, ideas that come through another person in another work. Remember, however, that these are already interpretations. Enjoy them for their own qualities — often they are a tremendous help in seeing old objects in new ways. But whenever possible, go to the source. Rely upon your personal response.

It is while you are working with colors and cutting shapes that many new ideas come. As you work on one piece of stitchery, ideas for others present themselves. Sometimes after a trip or a walk many ideas will be crowding in. Work them while the impressions are fresh. Start as many pieces as you will. Having eight or ten things under way at a time seems reasonable to me. There will be times when you can sew on one while another has less appeal. Sometimes a piece has to "rest" awhile, and when you return to it after a few weeks it is easier to see what is needed.

A value of working on several stitcheries at a time is the way in which one enriches another. You will develop something in one which might be modified for another, or will offer ideas for new ways of working.

Plate 8. Caterpillar.

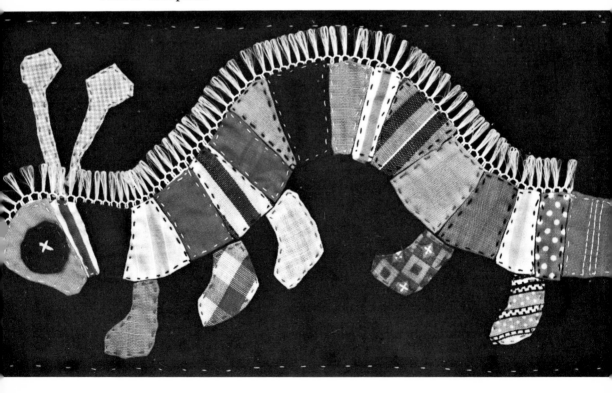

During those times when you are cutting and planning, and doing a tentative placement of shapes, you will most need to concentrate quietly. This may not be easy to do if the house is full of children's activities or time is pressing. Do your cutting and designing when you have an hour or two of quiet or free time to devote to it. The sewing, which demands less decision-making, can be accomplished in small scraps of time or picked up when a friend drops by. Just thirty minutes of sewing a day will soon see pieces finished.

A final source of ideas awaits in the drawings of children. One woman who sewed exquisitely but who felt hesitant to do her own drawings made a quilt for her sons. Together the boys drew pictures of all the things they liked. She gave them papers the sizes of the blocks, and their drawings then fit into the needed size. The blocks depicted dump trucks, fire trucks, and bicycles — all things which they found exciting. Because children tend to simplify, the drawings were not too complex to be worked out in fabrics. Another mother took drawings which her children had made and produced them in fabric for pillows to be given the grandparents as a special gift. The children's names as they had signed them became a part of the design, and the ages were added. My daughter, playing with fabric scraps, arranged fabric pictures which were machine sewn for her into pillows for her room. At eight, she is now learning to use the sewing machine herself and will soon be sewing her own. Some of her ideas shown in Figure 12 would lend themselves to appliqué.

A special trip or a favorite story may inspire a child with ideas for an appliqué design. This can be worked out as a joint project, with the child doing the drawing and cutting, and the mother or teacher helping on the sewing. Because of the kind of wear pillows receive (particularly in children's rooms) they need a well-sewn edge. For a panel, where wear is minimal, the child will probably prefer to do the sewing.

The use of children's drawings has most value for the child himself. It is a possible source for adults to draw from, on occasion, but would be limiting if it were the only source. Doing things for or about children can be as rewarding as working directly with their drawings. Plates 5, 6, 7, and 8 show block designs from a quilt made for a child. Plate 9, "Jungle Gym," was done for children but it is my own design. "Train," Color Plate VI, was made for my son who is depicted standing with his teddy bear, waving to the engineer. Looking out the train window are his playmates. This panel was a favorite for several years.

All the things you have done and seen provide sources for ideas. Subjects may come from memory and recollection, they may be right outside your kitchen window, or perhaps they come from your study and imagination. All the details of your surroundings — the countryside, the buildings, the flowers, the fields, and the people — offer possibilities for stitchery. You need only open your eyes and look.

Plate 9. Jungle Gym. 30 by 54 inches. Leap-frogging and running children fill a decorative panel. Details of faces and flowers are hand sewn, while larger fabric shapes are machine appliquéd.

2

DEVELOPING THE IDEA:
COLOR, DESIGN, AND PATTERN

The Properties of Color
The Elements of Design
The Importance of Pattern

Color, design, and pattern are inseparable parts of a single piece of stitchery. They are the ingredients that blend into a whole and it is as difficult to isolate one from the other as it is to extract an egg from cake batter. We can, however, examine them separately before combining them.

This examination of each will serve as a general guide. It will not answer every question that may arise regarding color, design or pattern, but it will offer a basis on which to make decisions.

Clustered together, colors are more congenial if (like humans) they share a common interest. People may assemble because they work in the same office, because they are members of the same family, because they all drive ancient cars or raise prize camellias. Some single element brings them together. There is at least one unifying factor. A common factor may also help in combining colors, though it is simpler with colors because each has just three basic variables. Unless one of these variables is shared by the group, they will not always "get along" in a harmonious way.

The information that helps you combine colors in a pleasing way also helps you in combining colors to deliberately make them clash or startle. You can ignite the explosion (much as with personalities) by combining certain ones — by seating the incompatible ones together.

THE PROPERTIES OF COLOR

There are three factors to every color: hue, value, and intensity. The study of these properties is never dull if you think in terms of colors instead of definitions.

HUE

This word refers simply to the color by name — red, yellow, green, blue, and so on. If five colors are used together, each having in it some yellow, a degree of harmony is achieved. This is one of the simplest and surest ways of combining color. The sharing of a common hue will bond the colors.

When you wish to work with a particular color as the dominant one — for example a bright blue — then try calling on its next-of-kin. A series of related blues will combine to give a stronger color effect than will the repeated use of a single blue. In working with the blue, push it to its limits in all directions. Add another blue, with a little red in it, as a blue violet, or purple. Or take the blue to a blue-green. Lighter and darker blues may be added. Whichever direction you go, some variations on your color choice will add a richness. In "Scarlet Garden," Color Plate XV, the multiplicity of reds produces a total effect more intense than any one red could have been.

Depending upon the colors which surround them, two colors sharing a hue will look more or less related. A red and an orange, when surrounded by blues, will look similar. But if only reds and oranges are used, the differences between them become more evident. The hues appear to change according to their color environment.

In "Urban Flower," Color Plate XIX, the variation of reds within the large petal shapes produces a more brilliant effect than just one red could have done.

When colors are very close, they blend. As they move further apart, they tend to clash. That is, they become further opposed on the color wheel. Knowing a basic color wheel structure may help here. Red, yellow, and blue, the primary colors, are spaced at the points of a triangle. Between these are the secondary colors which result from mixing primaries; orange between red and yellow, green between yellow and blue, and violet between blue and red. Colors directly opposed on the color wheel, as blue and orange, or yellow and violet, will clash most. Those adjacent clash least, or tend to blend.

The color wheel is not essential to a study of color, but it is helpful in understanding color relationships. Many color wheels are limited in that they refer to colors in terms of hue alone. Value and intensity, which are equally important, are often ignored. Think of the wheel especially in terms of hue, and remember that value and intensity also must be taken into consideration.

Yellow and yellow-green obviously flow together, blend, or bond themselves into a unit. Yellow and blue-green have little in common and though the blue-green contains some yellow, they are barely "kissing cousins." It is possible to move smoothly from yellow to blue-green, however, by advancing step-by-step through the colors between them. In "Indian Summer," Color Plate VIII, a wide range of colors is used but each leaf color is related to the color next to it. In this way, the color moves smoothly from yellow to red, from red to blue. Another example

Plate 10. Two in the Bush. 21 by 52 inches. Value contrasts which are not apparent in the Color Plate of this panel become clearly evident when it is reproduced in black and white.

of "pushing" a color to its limits may be seen in "Thicket," Color Plate VII. Here the tone is predominantly blue-green. The background color and all large shapes contain either one or both of these colors. These colors are then pushed gradually out of the major hue group — so far, in fact, that both red and yellow are used. Because the blue-green remains so dominant, the extensions to the other primaries remain as accents.

In areas where the blue-green moved toward the blue, leaves of blue-violet appear. Over the blue-violet come the magenta and red. These accents are used in line, but not in large areas. The magenta and red lines are not used over greens, where the contrast in hues would be most extreme. When they are near the greens, the red turns to an orange.

The same procedure was used in reaching for the yellow. Shapes move from blue-green to green, then yellow-green, and yellow lines cross these. Here again, the yellows are superimposed onto the greens — they do not reach out over blue where the contrast would be too great. The transition is gradual and smooth, giving the total panel a unifying color, with a heightening color effect in various areas. The accent colors, or those which are furthest away from the dominant, appear in the smallest amounts.

Color is one of the most exciting and appealing aspects of stitchery. But it must be remembered that hue is only one part of color. Until we can select colors by value and intensity as easily as we do by hue, we rarely make most effective use of it.

Plate 11. Frost Garden. 4 by 5 feet. Transparent and opaque fabrics are combined in this machine appliqué on heavy upholstery fabric.

VALUE

This term refers to the amount of dark or light (black or white) in a color. A color with white added is a lighter value; with black, a darker value. A variety of unrelated hues can better be combined if they are similar in value. We often do this without realizing that we are combining values. In spring, lightweight fabrics may appear in pastels. Red, blue, green and violet, with white added, become pink, baby-blue, pale green and lavender. As pastel colors, they can then be combined into a harmonious total. They share a common element of white. Printed fabrics often use a variety of hues, all in pastel or light value.

In the fall, fabrics tend to be darker in value. Orange-reds, with black added, become rusts. Summer greens turn to olive greens, bright yellows to golds. The dark value colors combine well, again because they have something in common. Value tends to add or subtract weight. Light value colors appear cooler for summer. In fall, the added weight of dark values seems heavier or warmer.

Any work photographed in black and white is reproduced in terms of value. Plate 10 shows a detail of "Two in the Bush." Here, with all the reds, oranges, and pinks omitted, we see the panel in darks and lights. This pattern of dark and light is much stronger than you might guess when you see it reproduced in close reds, Color Plate I.

When a color does not seem to "work" with others, or the relationship is not satisfactory, it is often the value that is disturbing rather than the hue. Plate 11, "Frost Garden," is a panel of beiges and soft whites with some darker values emerging at the lower edge. The close value range is apparent when the hanging is reproduced in black and white.

Colors are not necessarily always combined with related values. If the range of hues is limited — for example, an assortment of yellows — then a great range of values may be used. This was done in "Spring Flowers," Color Plate V, using whites, yellows, and gold. The range of hues is strictly limited, but the value change from white to deep gold makes a relatively strong contrast. Plate 12 shows this same panel in black and white. Value changes can add a vitality or movement to a close hue range.

The detail in Plate 13 shows a panel that uses extremely strong value contrasts. In this case, yarn stitches are used to provide a transition from solid dark to solid light. The areas of line provide a middle value. The value contrasts here, being great, make a very active, strong design.

An understanding of value will be of greatest help in working with color. This element is too often overlooked. It is so easy to identify colors by hue that we must learn to look at them in terms of value.

Plate 14 shows the value change in "Scarlet Garden." The same panel also appears in Color Plate XVI. Plate 13 appears in color in Color Plate XII. By comparing each with its counterpart in color, you can better understand value.

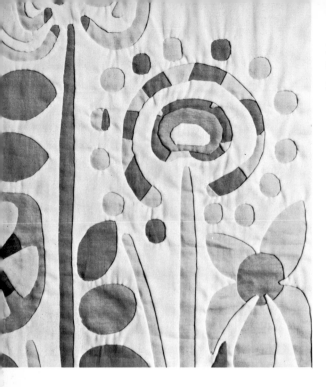

Plate 12. Detail of **Spring Flowers.** Fabrics are stacked four deep for this cut-through work which is then sewn with the blind stitch. Its value changes become evident here when seen without color.

Plate 13. Detail of **Ophelia's Flowers.** A transition from solid darks to solid lights is accomplished through areas of heavy yarn stitching.

INTENSITY

The third property of color refers to brilliance. To reduce the intensity of a color, another hue is usually added. For example, a drop of green added to red rapidly dulls the intensity of the red. It is no longer as bright a red as it was to begin with. A color is dulled in intensity fastest by the addition of its opposite on the color wheel. Red will dull green — violet will dull yellow — blue will dull orange, etc. If this is carried further, with equal amounts of the two colors, eventually you arrive at a minimum intensity, dull color. This may be a muddy or a dull grey-brown. A low intensity color does not "carry" well; that is, it does not show for a great distance. It tends to recede, to stay in the background. High intensity colors are bright, and tend to move forward.

It is not essential to know how to mix colors in order to successfully combine them in fabrics. Mixing colors in paints is often a great aid in helping us to see colors, however, or to determine the make-up of a particular color. Once having mixed colors in paints you can more easily recognize the color ingredients in fabrics. In "Festival," Color Plate XVIII, the colors are all bright. They are of similar intensity, although every hue is used. In the "Foods and Wines" panel, Color Plate X, a low intensity is used for the background. Bright colors are spotted over all, creating a decorative, active pattern.

As you work with colors and watch for their varying intensities, you will begin to recognize them more easily. It will aid you in the deliberate selection of colors.

These three dimensions — hue, value, and intensity — are in effect every time you use color. We often combine colors effortlessly, without consciously trying to relate them. We find certain combinations to have pleasing effects and this influences further choices. Other combinations jar or clash, and when this is the desired effect, we learn through having "found" that relationship. It will help to know why some effects are more satisfying, especially for those occasions when you may wish to reproduce a similar spirit with new subject matter.

In selecting colors to work with, concentrate on only one aspect at a time. If you are using a number of different hues, then limit the variation in value and intensity. If you are using strong value contrasts, then keep the range of hues narrow. This will simplify the work initially, and as you continue working you will gain confidence and competence in handling more complex ideas. The added complexity of working with all three dimensions adds to the challenge and the excitement in using color.

Work with colors you like. Many people find that their marked preferences are evident in their homes and in their clothing, or that their favorite colors are related to the objects — as bright, sunny yellow or foliage green. If you sew, go through your fabric remnants and you will probably find a series of related colors. Perhaps in that assortment you will have a predominance of bright, intense, gay colors or a collection of soft pale colors. If your home is essentially greens and golds, that preference may serve as a beginning. But choose colors you personally respond to — they will be easier and far more pleasurable to work with.

It is not necessary to remember all these details regarding color. It is better to select your colors by preference, and continue working as long as the results are pleasing. When you have difficulty, however, that is the time to refer back to this section and review. Let it be a guide to finding the source of difficulty.

Plate 14. Scarlet Garden. 15 by 18 inches. Compare this reproduction to Color Plate **XVI** and note the value changes, particularly in the embroidered details.

Figure 13. A series of apples, reduced to the simplest forms.

THE ELEMENTS OF DESIGN

Design in stitchery refers to the shapes and forms selected to suggest an idea, an attitude, or a feeling, and to the arrangement or organization of those shapes and forms. The shapes and arrangements may represent objects, or become abstractions. A single idea can be depicted in a great variety of ways. An arrangement of forms may suggest a lively, spirited and playful feeling, or it may suggest stability, weight, and an enduring quality. A bird, for example, might be blocky, heavy, sturdy, and angular in form, or it may be feathery, delicate, and fragile. The designing, the determining of the form, communicates to the viewer a kind of bird, or an attitude about it.

The arrangement of the forms determines the strength of the design. A compactly organized design invites a response very different from that of a delicate, linear design. A series of lines arranged in a radiating pattern would produce a tight, strong, unified design. The same lines, scattered, may produce a chaotic or haphazard effect. The design is determined by what you want to say, what attitude you hold toward the idea; and you select and arrange forms accordingly.

Generally, the most difficult aspect of design is that of simplifying. To do so requires clarity of purpose or singleness of idea. Children's paintings often surprise us with their refreshing clarity; they leave little question as to what is important. Simplifying gives dominance or emphasis to the most important element.

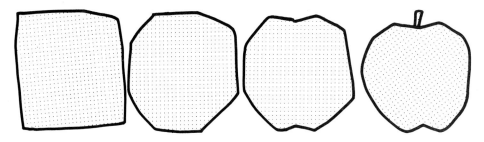

Figure 14. Let forms emerge gradually from your fabric. Snip and cut until you arrive at the desired shape.

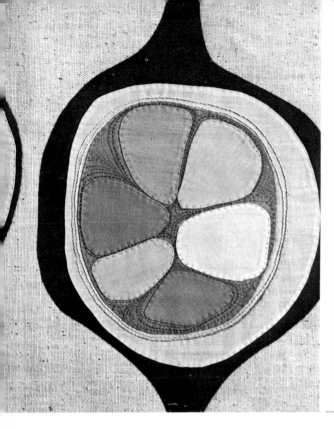

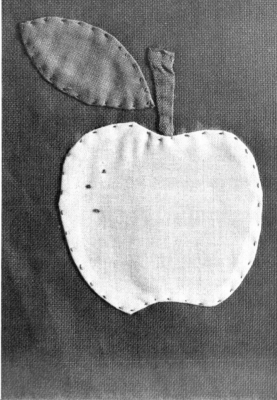

Plate 15. Detail of **Seed Pods.** The lines of running stitches take their directions from the appliquéd forms.

Plate 16. In this apple design for a table napkin, the simplest forms are used, with the appliqué stitch providing a decorative element.

Seeing objects in terms of their simplest shapes will help. Avoid too many details in your basic design. Select just two or three large shapes; the small forms will come later. Figure 13 suggests apples through minimum use of detail. Each has been simplified to one or two basic forms.

To cut these forms, first take a piece of fabric which is somewhat larger than you wish the finished piece to be. Temporarily fold the edges under to help you determine size. Then trim gradually until you arrive at the form you want. Remember that the shape is already there in the fabric. You need only trim away the excess. See Figure 14.

Keep all shapes simple. Reduce each piece to approximate a rectangle, circle, or square, if that helps. A tree may be represented by a rectangle and just the repeat of a leaf shape. Do not concern yourself with "realism." A cloth leaf has little resemblance to an actual leaf anyway, so there is no need at that point to concern yourself with more than the essence. Work in terms of your total design, letting the natural form inspire you but not enslave you.

Forms and shapes used together are combined much like colors. Each is related to the others which surround it. Together they produce a total. The line drawing in Plate 15 shows how one shape takes its form from another. Design is probably the most personal part of your work. The shapes you choose to represent an object, or the forms you select for a design must be yours. They will be the result of all your interests and your observations. They take form only when your efforts transfer them into an area of color.

Do not concern yourself about an ability to draw. If you feel you "can't draw," select ideas first which do not demand too much of you. Plate 16 is a simple design of just three pieces. The drum in Plate 17 requires little drawing, as it is composed of rectangles and circles. In "Island," Plate 18, the trees are formed of just two cut pieces. These shapes are all simple to cut and easy to sew. "The Village" in Plate 19 is a collection of small squares and rectangles. A few shapes used over and over in variation do not demand great skill. The shapes may be placed tentatively, then moved and rearranged over and over until a happy design is achieved.

Plate 17. A quilt block, composed of simple rectangles and circles, requires little in the way of drawing ability.

Plate 18. Island. 22 by 29 inches. Objects are reduced to their simplest forms so that trees become just trunks with a suggestion of the leaves. Stitches provide the details in this hand-sewn piece on wool.

Many beginners become too easily discouraged. Trying two or perhaps three times to cut a particular shape, they give up. It is only with practice that it comes easy. I still find I must sometimes cut a shape four or five times, finally discarding it. These first cuts are like rough sketches in which you block in shapes, suggesting forms quickly. Then the refining can begin. Too often the difficulty lies not in the cutting but in anticipating or visualizing the desired shapes.

You may benefit from first sketching or drawing your ideas on paper. This helps crystallize your thoughts, but to then work rigidly or directly from the drawings may be more of a hindrance than a help. In my own work, while I often draw, I do not cut the fabrics from a drawing, nor do I make patterns. They seem to me to be too unrelated and unnecessarily limiting. Let your scissors serve you as pencil, sketching with them as you snip and cut.

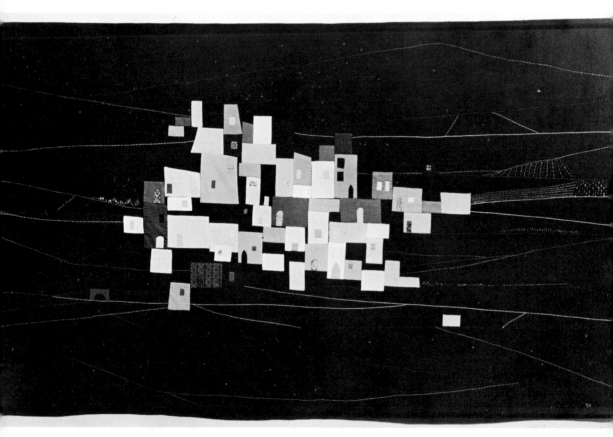

Plate 19. Village. 30 by 52 inches. In quiet repose, the simple squares and rectangles are varied and repeated to produce a concentrated pattern. Here cottons are used on wool, with couching for the lines.

Figure 15. Leaf shapes result from the collection of many small lines into patterns.

To work out in color what was originally planned in black and white line involves many changes. It is best to let the color and form emerge together from the fabric. A drawing for your design will simply divide a sheet of white paper into areas through the use of line. When this is transferred to fabric, and areas change to color, the emphasis will inevitably change. What was an unimportant shape on the sketch may, depending upon its color and surrounding colors, become centrally important. I would suggest then that you look at your sketch in terms of the idea. Then put away the drawing and work directly with the fabric.

THE IMPORTANCE OF PATTERN

Pattern is produced through the arrangement of many small shapes to produce new shapes. A series of lines, forming a pattern, can produce a leaf shape. A series of these leaves, placed in a pattern, can produce a tree shape. Small lines and forms combine and develop to form larger shapes. It is this pattern within pattern that gives a design richness and complexity. Figure 15 suggests patterns of lines or shapes which combine to form new shapes.

Sometimes a large appliqué area is best broken down into a series of smaller forms. These are again divided until a series of stitches forms a final pattern. Plate 4, "Eve's Apple," suggests one way in which a large area can be broken down into a pattern of smaller shapes, then into patterns of stitches.

In the small "Butterfly" in Plate 5 the stitches form an edge pattern. In "Blue Leaf," Plate 20, the small stitches which hold down the heavier threads form a secondary pattern. French knots in "Festival" and "Bong Tree," Color Plates XVIII and XIV, serve not only as a means of appliqué, but also as another pattern superimposed on the cut forms. Pattern is also developed through the use of color. To think of this principle as "patter" may describe it as well.

Color, design, and pattern are inseparable parts of a single piece of stitchery. Once combined it is difficult to distinguish one from the other. It is possible, however, to control the amounts put into the total. When one area is emphasized, then another must be subdued. If color becomes the dominant and active element, then design and pattern may be kept to a less prominent role. Concentrate on only one area at a time, especially in the beginning.

For the person to whom the concepts of applied design, pattern, and color are new, do not be discouraged. Many of the comments on these areas will take on further meaning as you work. Avoid looking for magic rules to rely on. Refer back to these comments when you feel a need for help. Each time you work with color, design, and pattern, the preceding comments will mean more. You can only learn by working, and your mistakes have as much to offer as your successes. There are no rules, no rights or wrongs, in the use of these elements. The most appropriate combinations, the most satisfying shapes, the most pleasing arrangements usually result from personal preferences in terms of the idea, the feeling, and the craftsmanship.

Plate I. Two in the Bush. 21 by 52 inches. Hand sewn embroidery details enhance this machine appliqué panel.

Plate II. Detail of **Two in the Bush.** Knitting yarns are used for the stitching and the French knots.

Plate III. Spice Garden. 13 by 24 inches. A cut-through stitchery using cotton percales.

Plate V. Spring Flowers. 18 by 18 inches. Cut-through stitchery using five layers of fabric.

Plate IV. Detail of **Thicket.** Hand couched lines of yarn spread out over a machine appliqué on upholstery fabric.

Plate VI. Tom's Train. 24 by 54 inches. Panel for a boy's room, sewn in hand appliqué on a variety of cotton fabrics.

Plate VII. Thicket. Mural 5 by 11 feet. Large areas of appliqué are of cotton percales, with yarn-stitched lines adding color accents.

Plate VIII. Indian Summer. 32 by 46 feet. Rich fall colors combine with hand embroidered details on this wool backing fabric.

Plate IX. Two Trees. 35 by 45 inches. Velour, satin, felt, and wool are combined to give strong textural contrasts to this very simple design.

Plate X. Foods and Wines. 3 by 6 feet. One of a series of panels for a restaurant. A wide variety of fabrics is used along with hand-stitched details.

Plate XI. Ophelia's Flowers. 2 by 5 feet. Concentrated areas of hand stitching overlap areas of appliqué.

Plate XII. Detail of **Ophelia's Flowers.** The closely spaced couched lines soften the transition from dark to light.

Plate XIII. Castle. 12 by 14 inches. Cottons are hand appliquéd to cottons with a blind stitch in this simple arrangement of rectangles.

Plate XIV. Bong Tree. 20 by 26 inches. Felt shapes are appliquéd to a felt background with French knots.

Plate XV. Detail of **Scarlet Garden.** Cut-through technique is here combined with freely used embroidery stitches.

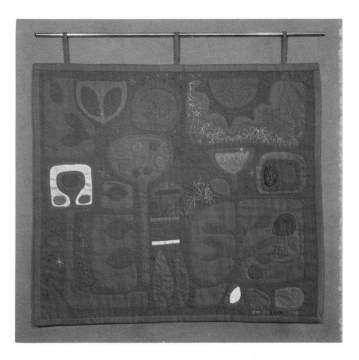

Plate XVI. Scarlet Garden. 15 by 18 inches. Four layers of percale in related reds are stacked for this cut-through appliqué.

Plate XVII. Extravagant Needle. 22 by 24 inches. Embroidery stitches of yarn, floss, and mercerized thread combine on a wool backing fabric.

Plate XIX. Urban Flower. 36 by 40 inches. Machine appliqué using burlap, satin, cotton, and canvas on a wool background.

Plate 20. Blue Leaf. 9 by 10 inches. A net form suggests an area over which couched lines of thread and floss produce a pattern.

3

GIVING THE IDEA FORM

Tools and Equipment Needed
Determining Whether to Sew
  by Hand or Machine
The Basic Appliqué Stitches
The Basic Embroidery Stitches

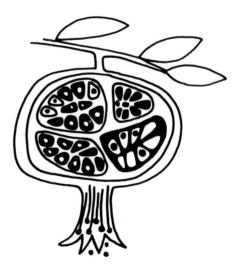

Fabric shops today offer a visual festival. Not only is the range of colors extensive, but the weaves and fibers are unlimited. Acrylic canvas in permanent colors makes it possible to use stitchery out-of-doors. Felts as wide as six feet are available in brilliant colors. Cottons and percales, at reasonable prices, cover a full range in weights and colors. Synthetics and wools are washable. You are not limited by the availability of the material.

For hand sewing, I suggest starting with a background fabric of cotton or a finely woven wool. It may be easier for you to use a fabric in which the threads are smooth and even, avoiding a nubby or textured weave. For the appliqué fabric a cotton percale or broadcloth will work well. Not only is there a tremendous range of colors available, but these fabrics are easy to handle. If you have scrap fabrics available, these are a good supplement, but start by selecting some new ones. A new cotton has some sizing in it, which makes it easy to turn edges under. It can be creased with the fingernail, and holds its shape better.

In buying fabrics, first select a background color appropriate to your idea. The appliqué colors are then chosen in terms of the background. This is easier than the reverse.

Wool is a nice backing material, as it offers so little resistance to the needle. The more tightly woven the fabric, of course, the more difficult to sew through. Therefore canvas, drill, and tarpoon cloth are harder to use. Wool, linen, percale, broadcloth, and felt all work well as backing for hand sewing. A fabric too loosely woven, as monks cloth or burlap, is not satisfactory for fine sewing. There is not enough "body" for threads to be held tight. However, for yarn stitches or to apply felt, either would be fine.

Allow three or four inches at each edge if you intend to stretch the panel over a board or frame. An extra one or two inches will be ample for hemming. Ways to bind fabrics and hang them are discussed at the end of this chapter.

Assuming you are starting on a piece that is modest in scale, such as a pillow or hanging, you will need only small amounts of fabric. Just one fourth yard of ten different colors would be a total of only two and a half yards. The leftover pieces are kept, and as you buy new colors for new projects you will soon develop a full range palette. If you are given fabrics, it may be necessary to wash them for shrinkage or color-fastness. Most new fabrics will not shrink or fade, and it is not necessary to wash them before using.

TOOLS AND EQUIPMENT NEEDED

Most homes contain all the essential tools for hand stitchery. Besides your fabrics, you will need an assortment of needles, threads, pins, and scissors. The size of the needle depends somewhat upon your own preference. It is also determined by the fabric on which you are working. The coarser or heavier the fabric, the stronger your needle must be. On a very light or delicate organdy or silk, I like a needle with a very fine shaft. Sometimes milliner's needles, when they can be found, will work well. It is not a strong needle, being very slender and long, but it sews through the finest fabrics with ease. Embroidery needles, having larger eyes for threading, are somewhat heavier and work well on wool. A package of assorted (3 to 9) embroidery needles will fill most needs and can be used for flosses of various weights. A package of assorted round-eye needles will serve for almost all appliqué. Try several and decide what length of needle works best for you. A darning needle, or a tapestry needle will be needed for yarn work. Both are heavy needles with large eye openings for yarns. The darning needle has a pointed, sharp tip. The tapestry needle is blunt.

Cotton mercerized thread is the best for appliqué. It comes in a wide range of colors and is smooth and strong. As you purchase fabrics, also

Plate 21. Detail of **Seed Structure.** Mercerized threads form the delicate embroidery in this detail.

select several threads to use with them. And here is a place to begin to expand on your colors. If your fabrics are reds, select threads in red, wine, orange, and magenta. When you use a running stitch, then use a thread color that is close but does not match. From a distance the thread and fabric will blend, but at close range the difference will add a vibrancy to the stitches. This minute color change is one of those details which will add interest to the design.

You may use mercerized thread for embroidery. Plate 21 shows thread used this way. In Plate 22, mercerized thread and embroidery floss were combined. You may wish to add an assortment of embroidery floss.

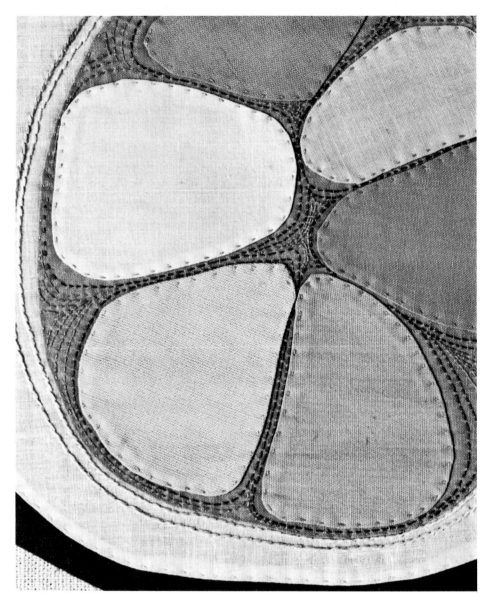

Plate 22. Detail of **Seed Pods.** Embroidery floss gives more weight to the circles that outline the larger shape. Mercerized thread is used for the fine lines which surround the seeds.

These, used two or three strands at a time, give a heavier line which carries color more than mercerized thread. Plate 23 shows the use of embroidery floss.

Yarns, too, should be added. If you know weavers or knitters, ask them for leftovers. A twenty-inch piece of yarn is of little value to either, but in stitchery it may be an ample supply. Unless you need specific colors in large amounts, it is unnecessary to buy skeins of yarn. A few yarn shops sell small "swatches" of yarns, and these are excellent to buy for use in

Plate 23. Gold Leaf. 9 by 12 inches. Heavier lines in the panel are sewn from embroidery floss, couched in place with sewing thread.

Plate 24. Yarns provide large bold lines for the embroidery, with smaller accents of mercerized thread and floss.

stitchery. Also available are the small amounts of yarn packaged for darning. Figure 24 uses yarn for embroidery, along with small areas of thread and floss.

Dressmaker pins will be needed to hold cut pieces in place. In hand sewing, pinning is far superior to basting. In basting, you commit yourself to size and location. I feel it is much better to be free to shift and alter the position of pieces as you sew. As a piece is appliquéd, with turned edges making the shape smaller, the total effect changes. To compensate for this change in size the placement of shapes may have to be altered. The final determining of the form must occur beneath your fingers as you sew. Further, in basting it is easy to stretch bias edges of fabrics. Pinning keeps them flat until you are ready to turn them under and stitch them down. With machine appliqué, since fabrics are not turned under, the problem is not the same. Basting is helpful there.

Finally, you must have scissors that will cut. A four-inch blade is probably the most versatile, and if you are getting just one pair this will serve you best. If you can add a second, trimming shears that have two sharp points work well for cutting very tiny pieces and close curves. Few things are more discouraging than struggling with poor scissors that slide over thin fabrics and balk at the heavy.

If you are interested in machine appliqué, you will need a machine capable of zigzagging. I use the zigzag stitch for basting (Figure 16), then sew over the basted line with a satin stitch so that the line is completely covered as in Figure 17. The satin stitch is simply a zigzag in which the stitches are so close that no room is left between them. Without basting, the satin stitch tends to push the fabric ahead of the presser foot and it is difficult to keep it flat. Pieces are therefore pinned initially, then machine basted, and finally satin stitched.

When using the satin stitch, keep the stitches going at right angles to the cut edge. If necessary, lift the presser foot and turn the fabric slightly before continuing (Figure 18). Make right angle corners by stopping, lifting presser foot, and changing direction. This will give added strength at a corner and assure a neat, even edge.

An ornate or curved edge will be especially difficult to sew evenly unless you machine baste, since the bias gives more easily, and tends to stretch away from the presser foot. If your machine does not have the satin stitch capability, it is still possible to machine appliqué. A straight stitch, used backward and forward, can be used much like a drawn line over pieces of appliqué fabric. This will eliminate fraying to a large degree, but this is suitable only for wall hangings or similar use where wear is not a problem.

Figure 16. In machine appliqué the fabric should first be basted with an open zigzag stitch.

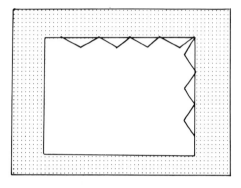

Figure 17. A machine satin stitch, or close zigzag, covers the basting stitch giving a firm, durable, appliquéd edge.

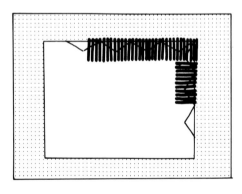

Figure 18. The machine stitches should run at right angles to the fabric. Lift the presser foot often to turn the fabric around corners or curves.

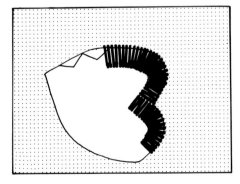

DETERMINING WHETHER TO SEW BY HAND OR MACHINE

Machine and hand appliqué are not, by any means, "opposite" ways of working. It is a matter of determining which is more appropriate in a given situation. Finer, more delicate fabrics seem to require a more delicate stitch. It seems fitting to hand sew on silk, fine percale, satin, or nylon. These fabrics are nice to handle and sew easily.

Upholstery fabrics, by contrast, are often so heavy that the edges cannot be turned under. Their weight or bulk may require that they remain flat. In this instance machine stitching may not be just preferable, but essential. Plate 25 uses machine appliqué on coarse fabrics as well as on the lighter weight birds. The decorative lines on the birds are sewn by hand.

Besides the matter of appropriateness, a second factor which may help you determine which is the better method is the size of your panel. As you work larger, the tendency is to also work with firmer or heavier fabrics. These are more easily sewn by machine. Light fabrics simply cannot hold the weight of much appliqué without sagging a little. Further, for large panels, machine appliqué will speed up the process and prevent the time spent from being excessive.

The largest machine appliqué panel I have sewn is "Flora," Plate 26. This piece, on a heavy upholstery ground, is just about the maximum size that can still be persuaded to pass under the arm of a home-model sewing machine. It is entirely machine sewn.

When working on large pieces, roll the fabric from each end, which keeps much of it out of the way as you work. It is not easy to maneuver these large pieces of fabric through the machine, but practice will help you learn the best ways of handling them.

Machine appliqué is not necessarily speedy. The satin stitch, done smoothly and well, is slow moving. It is, when it forms this solid line, very much like a drawn line. It is not limited in its use to appliqué. In "Two in the Bush" (Color Plate I), the heavy red lines are a continuation of the appliqué stitch. The stitch will have more or less strength depending upon whether the thread color contrasts with the appliqué fabric or blends with it.

A final determining factor in choosing the method of sewing is the use for which the work is intended. A pillow for a game room, family room, or patio may get hard use. In this case, machine appliqué would be more durable than hand work. The satin stitch can "give" a little on the bias. A hand-stitched line, when firmly sewn, is strong, but it may not survive pillow fights or continuous buffeting.

Plate 25. Birds. 2½ by 6 feet. A more startling contrast occurs between the heavy, strong textured darks and the white birds appliquéd onto a red backing material.

Plate 26. Flora. 5 by 11 feet. Cotton percales and broadcloth form a complex overlapping pattern in this mural.

Durability is not a primary consideration if you are doing a panel to hang on the wall. The main concerns are the fabrics and desired effect. The decision whether to sew by hand or by machine depends upon which is most appropriate for the fabric and for its use. You decide first what you are going to do, then seek the best way to do it. To decide on the technique first would be somewhat like deciding to travel by train — and then looking to see where the train was going. You must determine the destination first, and then look for the best way to get there. In my own work, there is an obvious preference for a certain use of the machine appliqué: satin stitch, outline, and drawing. However, the machine is extremely versatile, and I have only begun to explore its potentials for stitchery.

THE BASIC APPLIQUE STITCHES

Most of the difficult and complex stitches are merely variations on a few basic ones. It is better to be inventive with a few than become enamored of acquiring a great many. Intricate stitches put too much emphasis on the pattern of the stitch. Overall design is of much greater importance. The sewing is not the essential element — it is the means. Keep in mind that you are working with ideas, colors, and shapes. Stitches make this possible. They provide the way but they are not the purpose.

The two stitches that I find to be the easiest and most versatile for appliqué are the running (or simple) stitch and the blind stitch. Each running stitch keeps the fabric flat, adding a small scale stitch pattern at the edge. The blind stitch (hem stitch) is concealed, and it tends to make the fabric puff out, or stand away from the background.

The running stitch (Figure 19) is probably the first stitch anyone ever used in sewing, and its variations are unlimited. Knot the single strand of mercerized thread, drawing the needle through from the back. Then, dip the needle into both layers of fabric, and sew. The appearance of the stitches is controlled by the consistency of stitch length, and distance of stitches from the edge.

Consistency of stitch length comes largely through practice. If you have sewn much, you already have a "feel" for stitch length; that is, you can feel as you sew if the length is similar to the last stitch. To give the appearance of finer stitches, they need not necessarily be smaller. Rather, a smaller amount of the thread shows on top. In Figure 20 there are three

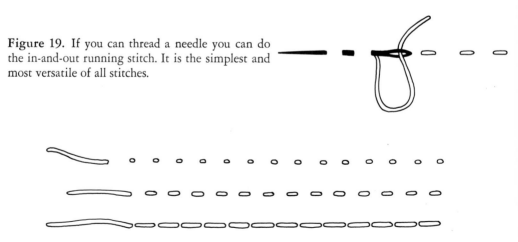

Figure 19. If you can thread a needle you can do the in-and-out running stitch. It is the simplest and most versatile of all stitches.

Figure 20. The running stitch varies according to how much of the thread is exposed and how much is hidden beneath the fabric.

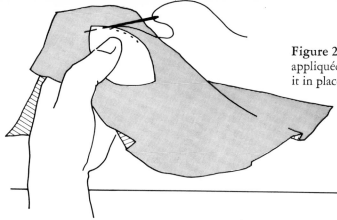

Figure 21. Hold the piece of fabric which is being appliquéd toward you, so that your thumb can hold it in place as you sew.

rows of stitching. Each shows stitches of the same length, but in one most of the thread is left showing on the surface. In another, the thread is half hidden, half on the surface. In a third, most of the stitch remains hidden.

To be sure that the edges of the appliqué fabric remain firmly turned under, keep stitches very near the edge. If they come in from the edge as much as a quarter of an inch, the fold may pop out, giving a frayed and unfinished edge. In sewing the appliqué, keep the cut shape towards you so that you sew on the outer edge. In this way, your left thumb can help to hold the fabric in place, as in Figure 21. Corners may be difficult until you have practiced on a few. To use a running stitch on a corner, fold under only one edge to begin with (Figure 22). Sew along this edge until you come to the hem line. Then turn under the second edge (Figure 23). Because the first side is already sewn down, the hem cannot pop out that side. Do not try to fold under both edges of the corner at once — it is much easier if they are taken one at a time. If the corner looks as if it

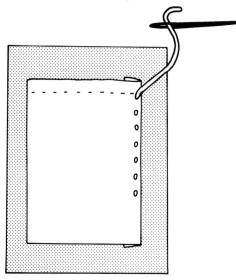

Figure 22. To appliqué a corner, first sew one edge all the way up to the hem allowance.

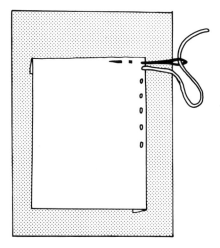

Figure 23. Using your needle to assist you in the folding, tuck the hem of the second edge under and continue stitching.

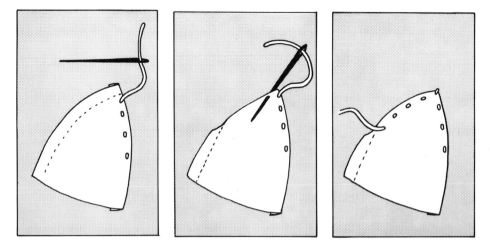

Figure 24. A pointed edge is the most difficult to appliqué. Sew one edge first. Then use your needle to turn under the second edge, taking a whip stitch at the tip to keep it from fraying.

might not stay, then take one or two whip stitches (an overcast stitch) on the corner, as in Figure 24. A whip stitch will always look better than a frayed corner. On an inside corner, the fabric must be clipped. Then use the same approach (Figure 25). Stitch down one edge, and do not fold under the second until you have reached the corner. It is almost always necessary to take a slip stitch on an inside corner. Plate 27 of the bird shows a slip stitch at the tip of the wing. Another is used at the beak

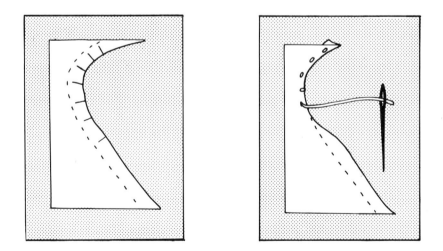

Figure 25. Inside corners can be appliquéd more easily if they are clipped on the curves. Take a whip stitch wherever needed to prevent fraying.

Plate 27. An ungainly little bird perches on this quilt block which uses the running stitch for appliqué as well as for the embroidery.

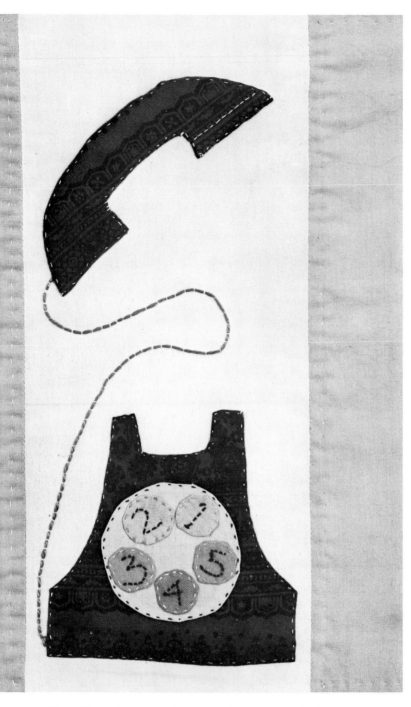

Plate 28. A child's telephone finds its way to a quilt block where a printed fabric was used to advantage.

to keep the corner from fraying. If you look closely at Plate 28 you will see that on the inside corners whip stitches are used to keep the corners secure. Here again, the slip stitch will always look better than a fraying fabric.

78

Plate 29. This pomegranate adds a bold red to a pink napkin. By overlapping shapes at the bottom, difficult-to-sew angles are avoided.

Some corners become such acute angles that they get very difficult to sew. In this situation, it is often possible to cut the fabric in such a way as to avoid the angle entirely. Plate 29 uses this solution. Had the points at the bottom of the pomegranate been cut all in one, it would have been

Plate 30. A watering can also becomes a quilt block, using only the very versatile running stitch.

hard to sew. Instead, each was cut separately which simplified sewing, and then the round shape overlapped these. Another example is seen in Plate 30. The spout and sprinkler of the watering can, cut in one piece, would be hard to sew. Cut separately, each is simple and the result is more effective. Plate 31 shows how shapes can be cut to overlap, and Figure 26 suggests ways to simplify the hard-to-sew angles.

Plate 31. The boy with his absurd grin decorates another quilt block. Many prints are used, and overlapping shapes eliminate the need to sew sharp corners.

Figure 26. As sharp corners are difficult to sew, eliminate as many as possible by overlapping cut pieces. The small x's on the cat mark hard-to-sew corners which can be eliminated.

Plate 32. Three Flowers. The matronly flowers stretch to their full height on a multi-colored background. While the layers of color suggest earth, sun-drenched air, and blue sky, it should also be admitted that my fabric supply was very limited, which accounts for the background piecing. A shortage of materials sometimes forces us into new solutions.

The running stitch, when used in strong contrast, produces a very active pattern. In "Three Flowers," Plate 32, the leaves are appliquéd in a dark thread which defines them on the background. In this same panel, the running stitch is used as a decorative addition where the background fabric is seamed. In this case then, the method of joining becomes an essential design element.

Practice the running stitch until you have mastered it. This is the only stitch you really need. All others will supplement it. When I first started work in stitchery I had only a meager background in sewing and the running stitch was the only stitch I knew. It was the only one needed for a long time. This same running stitch can also be used effectively for embroidery, and will be covered with the embroidery stitches.

Another common method of appliqué is the blind stitch. It is sometimes called the hem stitch or hidden stitch. To use this means of sewing, the thread should match the color of your appliqué fabric. As the thread is to be concealed, its matching color will camouflage it should it come through in places.

The doll's head in Plate 33 has features sewn with the blind stitch. The eyes and nose take on a rounded look, and stand slightly away from the face. Plate 34 is also sewn with the blind stitch. The edges of the appliqué look smooth and rounded. Inside curves, like those in the spoke-shaped flower, are easier to sew with blind stitch than any other way.

Plate 34. Blue Flowers. Blind stitch appliqué gives a puffy edge in this cut-through appliqué.

Plate 33. The eyes on this doll's head seem to pop forward. This is due in part to the wide-eyed expression and partly because of the use of blind stitch, which tends to make fabrics stand out. The mouth is a couched line.

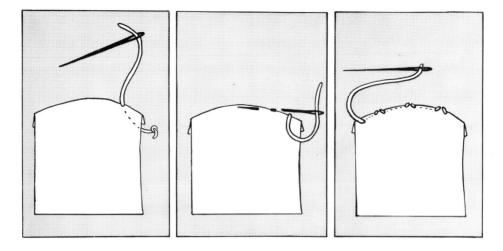

Figure 27. The blind stitch keeps a thread hidden in the folded hem of the fabric. The needle catches a thread of the background fabric, then dips into the fold.

To do this stitch, use a single thread and knot it at the end. Turn under the edge of the piece to be appliquéd, and draw your thread through from behind so that it emerges on the fold (see Figure 27). In stitching, the thread must now be hidden in one of two places — it will either be behind the backing fabric or within the fold of the piece you are appliquéing. Do not let the stitches, as they go from backing to appliqué, be long. They must go directly from one fabric to the other.

Corners are sewn much the same as they are with the running stitch. One edge is blind stitched until the turn under or hem allowance is reached. Then the piece is turned and the sewing continues on the next side, with the hem being turned under. The needle will serve as a very helpful tool in slipping the hem into place. It can reach into narrow seams more easily than fingers.

For occasional use, learn also to do a whip stitch. This is not a particularly attractive stitch, but it is a good tight one for reinforcing, for closing seams, or for heavy fabric. In this, the thread is brought through from behind. Then the needle moves above the appliqué piece to take its stitch, coming back up through the appliqué materials. The thread, in effect, binds the edge. It is a stitch commonly used in appliqué, but not, to my way of thinking, the preferred one. See Figure 28.

If you know the running stitch and blind stitch, adding the whip stitch when needed, you are well equipped for work in appliqué. While there are several other stitches which can be used, such as the buttonhole

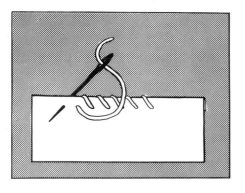

Figure 28. The whip stitch is a good strong stitch for binding edges.

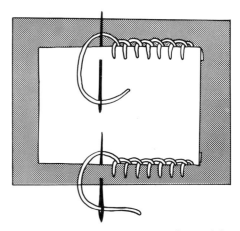

Figure 29. Buttonhole stitches can be used for appliqué with the stitches reaching either over the fabric or away from it.

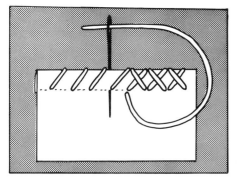

Figure 30. The cross stitch provides a decorative means of applying fabric firmly.

and cross stitch, they tend to put so much emphasis on the active stitch pattern that the appliquéd shape is overpowered. There may be times however when you intend to emphasize the line. Remember that these stitches become especially prominent, and will work best as borders, outlines, or in case of special emphasis. Two of these are illustrated in Figures 29 and 30.

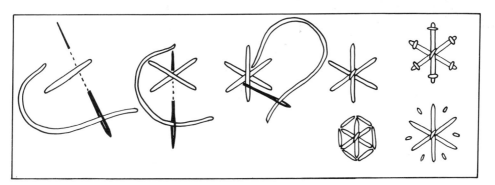

Figure 31. Stars are formed by crossing three stitches and attaching them with a whip stitch at the center. Do others crossing four or five stitches.

THE BASIC EMBROIDERY STITCHES

The embroidery stitches open whole worlds of possibilities. The use of needle and thread in embroidery is very much like the use of pen and ink. Think of your needle as a drawing tool which leaves behind it a fine trail of color. When working with appliqué, the embroidery tends to serve primarily as a means of enriching areas, adding details, and defining forms. Just a few basic stitches are all you need. As you sew, you will occasionally discover new stitches. I have "discovered" many myself, only to find that they are in reality very common stitches. So many of these complex stitches, each with its own name, are slight variations of others. If you look closely you will see that the feather stitch is really a buttonhole stitch that is not standing up straight.

The first and most basic of the embroidery stitches is the running stitch. This is identical to the stitch used in appliqué, (Figures 19 and 20), except that it is used "free" rather than confined to the edge of a

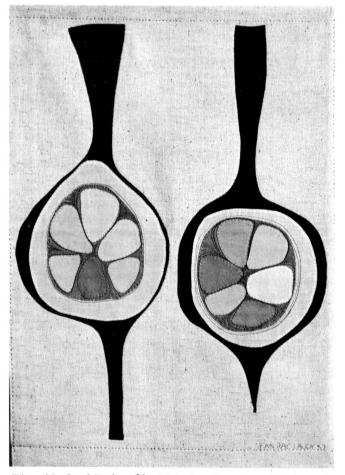

Plate 35. Seed Pods. 16 by 23 inches. Running stitch is used to provide an area of concentrated detail in this direct and simple design.

Plate 36. Detail of **Birds.** **A** running stitch is used much like a drawn line. Think of your needle as a pencil which leaves behind it a line of thread.

fabric. It uses either mercerized thread, embroidery floss or yarns. The length of the stitch determines whether it appears to be a solid line or becomes a trailing whisper of a line. Plate 35 shows the use of a running stitch to outline the seed pods and emphasize the small appliquéd pieces. The lines run over a background like drawn lines, changing in color as they move towards the center. In the "Birds," Plate 36, the embroidery on the birds' bodies uses the running stitch as a nearly solid line, picking up just a thread of the background. This lets the embroidery thread almost lie on the surface. A similar use is made of this line in the quilt

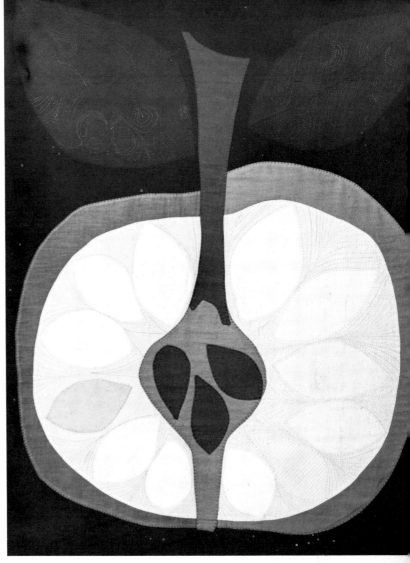

Plate 38. **Eve's Apple.** 23 by 30 inches. The needle becomes a drawing tool in this panel where the drawn lines of running stitch move over the leaves and the apple shapes.

block telephone seen in Plate 27. The phone cord is sewn with embroidery floss which catches just a single thread of the background material. The numbers are also sewn in this way and show how controlled a line can be achieved with this stitch. By contrast, a line more broken by the background is used in the detail of "Island," Plate 37. It is a continuation of the appliqué stitch, with about half the thread showing, half concealed. "Eve's Apple," Plate 38, uses the running stitch as a drawn line. New shapes emerge from combinations of lines.

Plate 37. Detail of **Island.** The sun sends out rays of running stitches, broken so that about half of each stitch is hidden. The same stitch is seen at the fabric edges where it is used as appliqué.

The running stitch, or single stitch, can be broken down into single parts. That is, one short stitch or line. This stitch can then be combined with others to make new stitches. In that same detail of "Island," we see this used on the branches of the cone-shaped tree. A single stitch at each side produces a suggestion of leaves. The running stitch is the only stitch used on that hanging, and it suggests how easily it can be varied and altered. The grasses are also a combination of several single stitches. Flowers on the round tree shown in Plate 18 are combinations of five or six single stitches which cross, with a final stitch to hold them together in the center (see Figure 31). In "Phrenology," Plate 39, single stitches are used side by side to produce complex areas of stitching. Used close enough together, they begin to take shapes of their own. Brought very close together they make what is called a satin stitch, but this is, after all,

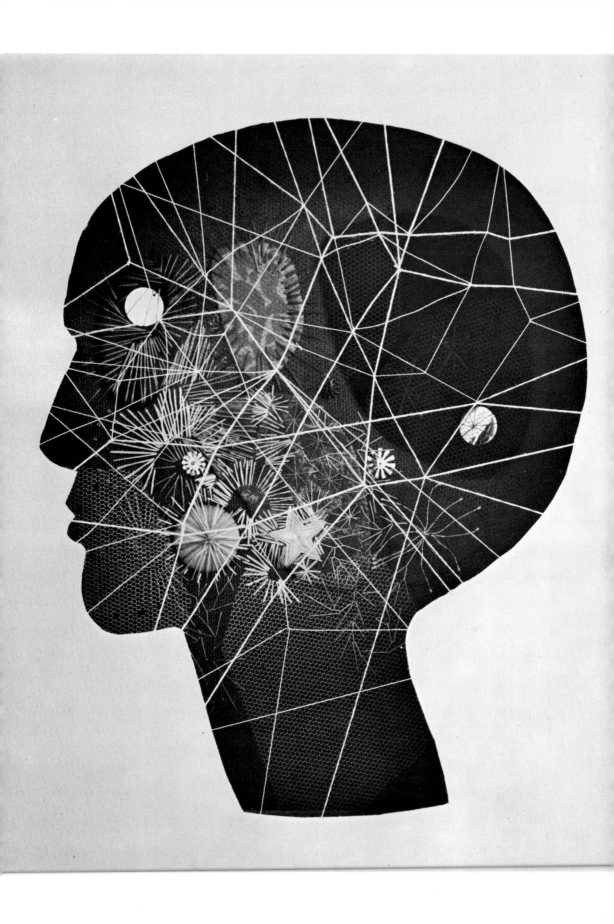

Plate 40. Yarns and flosses are used in satin stitch to provide areas of solid color.

a series of single stitches placed side by side. In Plate 40 those areas solidly covered by thread are satin stitched. Another use of the satin stitch is seen in the detail of Plate 41. How to sew this stitch is shown in Figure 32.

The second most valuable embroidery stitch is that of couching. The doll's head in Plate 33 uses couching for the eyebrows and mouth.

Figure 32. Satin stitch involves using a single stitch over and over. Placed side by side this stitch produces a solid area of thread or floss.

Plate 41. Detail of **Rare Seeds.** The smaller lines are crochet thread, tacked down or couched with mercerized thread. Satin stitches form solid areas of seeds.

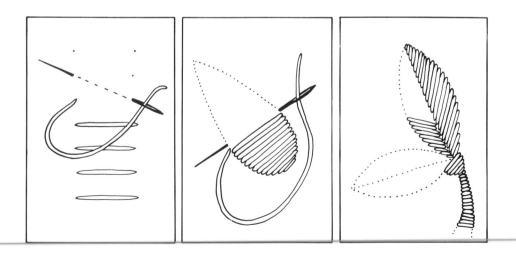

Couching involves tacking down one thread or yarn by using a second. First, the yarn or three to six strands of embroidery floss are pulled through from the back side of the fabric, just as if you were to start sewing. This is either knotted or tacked into place with the second thread, as in Figure 33. For a short line, as on the eyebrows and mouth of the doll, a large stitch is taken. Then the second thread comes through from behind and stitches the line into place. For very long lines, the yarn may be left loose on the surface, and turned or shaped as the stitching occurs. In "Rare Seeds," Plate 1 (frontispiece), the stems are sewn with heavy cotton yarn. It was drawn through, and laid flat until stitched down. The smaller lines, using a heavy crochet thread, started at the center. These crochet thread lines were tacked with the mercerized thread, and when the desired length was achieved, both threads ran through to the back side. The line pattern in Plate 34 is done entirely with couching, as is the line pattern on Color Plate XI. The threads attached to the backing range from a single sewing thread, to two or three strands of embroidery floss, all the way up to yarns and six strands of floss. Couching is often accomplished by using a backing stitch which runs at an angle to the yarns. This makes it least obvious and allows the yarn to lie flat. A variety of stitches can be used to make this line more decorative, as in Figure 34, but the simplest seems most appropriate to me, since the couched line is so similar to a drawn line.

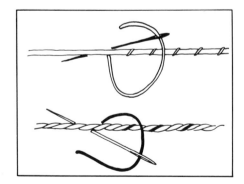 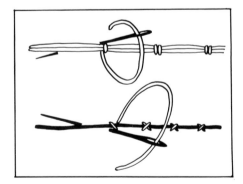

Figure 33. Couching is simply a means of attaching a yarn or thread to a surface by using a second thread. The couched line is much like a drawn line.

Figure 34. Couching can be made more decorative by using several yarns at once, or by attaching them with parallel or cross stitches.

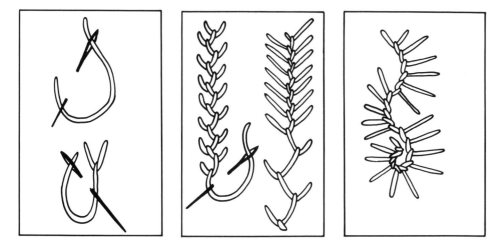

Figure 35. The "Y" stitch is the beginning of a feather stitch. By swinging the stitches from left to right and back to left, the feather is produced.

Figure 36. The feather stitch can be varied by changing the length of the stitches taken or by changing the space between stitches.

Figure 37. If stitches are repeated on one side, rather than swinging from right to left, you get a one-sided feather, which can easily be turned or twisted.

The third stitch is the feather, or "Y" stitch. The "Y" comes from its appearance when it is used singly rather than in a continuous line. Figure 35 shows the use of the single portion of the "Y" stitch. Made to join at either end, the stitches take on new forms. When used in continuous lines, this stitch takes on a "feathery look." To do the feather stitch, Figure 35, draw the thread through the fabric from behind. Pull the thread toward you, as in the sketch, and place the needle to the right of where the thread emerges from the fabric. Point the needle down, bringing it back up below the other two spots, forming a triangle. That is the basic stitch. The next stitch can be swung around to the left. To form the feather effect, the stitches are lengthened (Figure 36). If the stitch continues to be sewn from one side, it will swing around to form a circle, as shown in Figure 37. The stitch can be swung back and forth, stopped, and started over. The detail of "Scarlet Garden" in Plate 42 shows areas stitched with both the "Y" and feather stitches used freely. The feather stitch can be worked across the fabric from right to left, rather than toward you, although it is more difficult to visualize the finished appearance.

Plate 42. Detail of Scarlet Garden. A playful or free use of the feather stitch allows it to expand to fill any area. In the upper left, the "Y" stitch expands to fill the circle.

Plate 43. The accommodating chain stitch grows fat or thin, as you wish, and turns segmented corners.

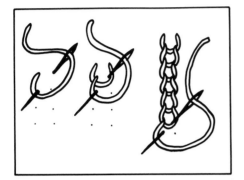

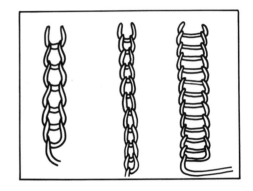

Figure 38. The chain stitch begins with the thread coming through the fabric at upper left, and being drawn down toward you. The needle is inserted to the right of the thread, and reaches diagonally across and below. The needle is pulled through but the stitch is not tightened until the needle is in place for the next stitch.

Figure 39. Chain stitches can be varied by altering the width or the length of the stitch. It can be made to fluctuate to fill areas of irregular size.

Very similar to the feather stitch is the chain stitch. The basic difference in this is simply in attaching the loop down with two threads instead of with one, as on the feather. Be sure to place the needle back into the fabric for the next stitch before pulling the last stitch tight. You form a square instead of a triangle. Details of "Extravagant Needle," Plate 43, show several versions of this stitch. Once you have mastered the elements of the stitch, then begin trying variations. Swing the stitches further apart, or make them long (see Figures 38 and 39). Many new stitches will present themselves through this open-ended approach.

These stitches, then, cover the basics: running and blind stitches for appliqué; and running, couching, feather, and chain stitches for embroidery. The final detail is the French knot, a simple and decorative addition. Knots form the dots on the watering can, Plate 31; and Plate 9 of the "Jungle Gym" uses dots along with the flowers across the entire panel. The knots are fast and easy. Both "Festival" and "Bong Tree," Color Plates XVIII and XIV, are covered profusely with French knots, done with three or four strands of embroidery floss. Knots can be varied in size by the weight of the threads or by the number of twists. Figure 40 shows the process. While a single strand of mercerized thread will pro-

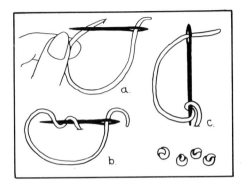

Figure 40. French knots add a decorative detail to any stitchery. When thread is pulled through from behind, it is wrapped once or twice around the needle. The point of the needle is put into the fabric and the thread drawn tight before the needle is pulled through. This will keep the knots tight on the fabric.

duce a tiny, delicate dot, the yarn will give a fuzzy ball of a knot. As the number of twists increases, it also becomes more difficult to take the stitch. Two, three, or four will work easily; more than that begin to get tight. Rather than make a knot in which five or six twists would be needed, switch instead to a heavier thread, or more strands of floss.

None of these stitches is difficult to do, though some may require more practice. You must be able to control the medium with which you work. Once you have mastered the stitches, then they will do anything you wish — until then, you may be their victim, having to accept the results without being able to determine them. As your skills develop, you will find how very flexible these few stitches are. With skill comes control and craftsmanship — without it comes sloppiness. Novel effects never compensate for poorly done work.

Some contemporary work in stitchery is executed with a complete denial of craftsmanship. Occasionally, a spontaneity and vigor are achieved which help to compensate for inadequate craftsmanship; but I feel that, provided the ideas are valid to begin with, you can achieve these qualities as well as a work that will survive dry cleaning or vacuuming without disintegrating.

PROJECTS IN APPLIQUE

BEGINNING PROJECTS

A first project should be simple, and not large in scale. Once you have started, your skills and ideas will grow so fast that you will soon want to move on. If you have committed yourself to a project that consumes too much time and energy, you may find your beginning work discouraging.

A pillow is an excellent piece on which to begin. It is small enough to finish in a short time, yet so versatile that it allows you to start off in whichever direction interests you most. It may be hand or machine sewn. Nearly any fabric can be used. A further advantage of the pillow is that it is a usable form. If, as you near completion of this first project, you feel that your color selection was not quite right, or that your design will improve on the next piece, you still have a pillow. And though you are not completely satisfied with the composition, you can plump it up, toss it into a chair and use it. With a panel or wall hanging, meant to be hung as you would hang a painting, you commit yourself to a more difficult task.

There are many directions in which your work can begin. Following are some projects which can appropriately be done with stitchery. With each is a description of approaches and comments which may be of some help.

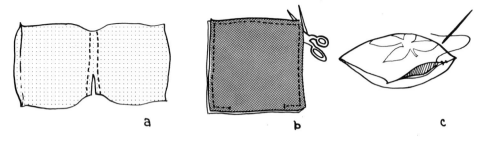

a   b   c

Figure 41. A bed pillow can be made into two throw pillows by first sewing two machine-stitched lines through the center, then by cutting between them (a). When you have finished your appliqué cover (b) sew as shown, trim, and turn. Then stuff the pillow form inside the pillow cover and whip stitch the opening to close it (c).

PILLOWS

If you are going to try a pillow first, it is important to decide where it might be used, for whom you are making it, or what object or idea you wish to appliqué. Then the fabrics and colors can be selected accordingly. It is important to make or buy the pillow form first. This may be filled with feathers, polyfoam, kapok, or Dacron. While pillows are usually available in department stores, it is not always easy to find one that is not already slip-covered. Decorators can order these for you, or you can make two throw pillows from a bed pillow. To do this, first machine sew two lines through the center of the pillow, as in Figure 41-a. Then cut between these lines. This will avoid the possibility of feathers or kapok flying out everywhere. Then bind or hem the cut edge. Those with sewing experience may prefer a boxed pillow, but a pillow made from two squares of fabric sewn at the edges will be the simplest for the beginner. This simple form makes a most attractive pillow. Once you have determined the size of your pillow, cut the pillow-top fabric one half inch larger at each edge, to allow for seams. Proceed then with the appliqué, working on the single flat piece of fabric. When the appliqué design is finished, place right sides of the pillow top together. Machine

Figure 42. Many subjects provide suitable appliqué for pillows.

sew on three edges, completing all four corners. If your design has a top and bottom (as a tree or a house) leave the opening at the lower edge (see Figure 41-b). Then clip corners and turn inside out. Stuff the pillow form inside your pillow cover and slip stitch or whip the seam opening by hand.

Although a circular pillow is very attractive, it should be boxed to hold its shape better. Zippers may be used to close pillow openings, but it is a very simple task to remove the few inches of hand-sewing if the cover needs to be washed or cleaned. When relaxing into a pillow, one can find the metallic feel of a cold zipper distressing.

Many simple appliqué designs can be worked for pillows. Figure 42 shows designs from a few. Plate 44 shows a pillow appliquéd to suggest a doll's body. It is felt, hand sewn to an upholstery fabric. On top of the pillow and attached to it is the doll's head, which is hand appliquéd, put together by machine, and stuffed. This combination brings us into another area of possible stitchery — that of dolls.

Plate 44. A doll's dress and arms are appliquéd to a pillow to suggest a body. Then the head is attached at the top.

Plate 45. Hair is made of cut felt strips and features are sewn with running stitch in this detail of the pillow doll.

DOLLS

Few materials are more suitable for dolls than fabric. Because fabric dolls are soft, they are particularly appealing. Being washable they are practical, though dolls of felt would require cleaning. The simplest form of doll allows for some imaginative and creative play on the part of the child, in contrast to dolls which walk, talk, cry, wet, and blink. A very simple form of doll, Figure 43, can be made from two simple shapes. Stuffed with dacron batting, the features may be sewn. Plate 45 shows the pillow doll in detail. Her face is felt, as are the features, sewn with running stitch. Another felt doll, with button eyes and a simple tube construction, is shown in Plate 46. The doll face in Plate 33 is cotton, with features blind stitched, and hair made from strips of cotton fabric. Dolls can also be for the amusement of grown-ups. There are many ways of making dolls which serve not only as decorative treasures, but as pillows as well.

Figure 43. Simple dolls can be made from two arch-shaped pieces of fabric. With fabric hands and feet inserted, faces can be appliquéd or embroidered.

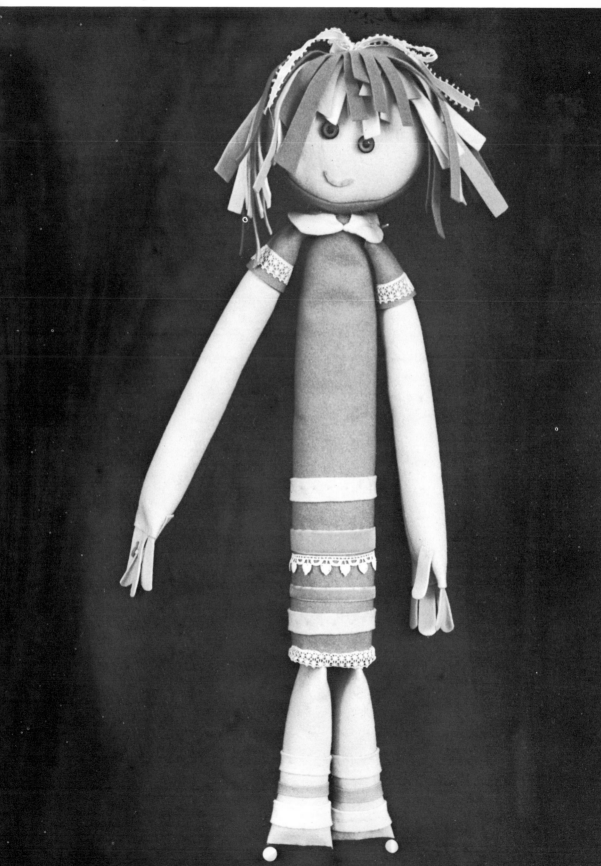

Pads for rockers, stools, and chairs are excellent projects for beginners as well as the more advanced. The process is similar to that used for pillows, except that it may be necessary to make the stuffed form if you have a chair of nonstandard size. A seat or pad provides a nice flat area on which to work your designs. The big advantage to appliquéing fabric for upholstery is the opportunity you have to fit the design to the chair. Dining room chair seats may be done in colors keyed to the room, or to special linens or place settings. Here again, as with pillows, the area being worked on is small, and easy to handle. The easiest way to determine the proper size for your specific need, is to remove any cover now on that piece of furniture and let it serve as a pattern. If you are cutting your own, allow ample fabric at the edges to draw the material around the chair seat.

For a stool or seat cover, where the fabric will be subject to sliding or wearing, be sure the stitches are firm and tight. Delicate fabrics, satins, or organdies would be inappropriate. Cottons stand up well as do closely woven wools or synthetic combinations. A chair seat for a child's rocker or stool will make it very special for him, giving him a lady bug or a flower to sit on. The appliqué pad can make a unique chair or seat from one that is very ordinary. See Figure 44.

Figure 44. Any child would delight in a pillow or pad for a special chair.

Appliquéd rugs are a little more difficult to handle, and I would not suggest this as a first project. Because of weight and size, they are more cumbersome to sew on and to move about. After you have gained some confidence in your work, however, you will find rugs an excellent project. Most of our homes could welcome a colorful area rug.

Felt makes a good backing as well as appliqué material. Plate 47 shows a felt rug, about three feet by six feet. For this, a piece of all wool, heavyweight felt provided the background. The applied designs are also felt, and range from gold through rust on an orange ground. Both the positive and negative portions of the cuttings are used. The lightest value in the photo is a yellow, shown at the right-hand end of the rug as a single cut shape, and at the other end as a negative shape, where the leftover pieces are used. This cuts down on the amount of materials needed, and develops a pattern of positive-negative areas. That is, the orange rug appears sometimes as the background and sometimes as the cut shape.

It is also possible to use a linen rug backing material on which to appliqué felt. This is much heavier, and is more difficult to machine sew, but gives a good weight to the rug. This backing is available through decorators, and in some department stores.

Felt rugs can be sewn either by hand or by machine. The satin machine stitch is extremely durable, and wool felt wears well. My real concern was that the tiny heels of women's shoes would go through the felt at the first step, but rugs which have been in use for several years show little in the way of wear. A felt rug serves best as an accent or area rug. If used over carpeting, it stays in place well. If it is used on a wood floor, or other smooth surface, a rubber backing should be added. This is available in the form of rubber pads, purchased by the running foot, or an ordinary rug pad can be basted on the back. There are also sprays available which can be applied to the under surface to keep the rug from slipping.

In machine appliqué, the most difficult thing about a rug is trying to turn the heavy fabric as you sew. Therefore, it may be easier to design a rug which simplifies this problem. In Figure 45, the rug on the left could be easily sewn. The one on the right could be machine sewn with the flower shape being added by hand. It is certainly possible to sew many complex shapes, but for your first attempt, keep it easy to handle.

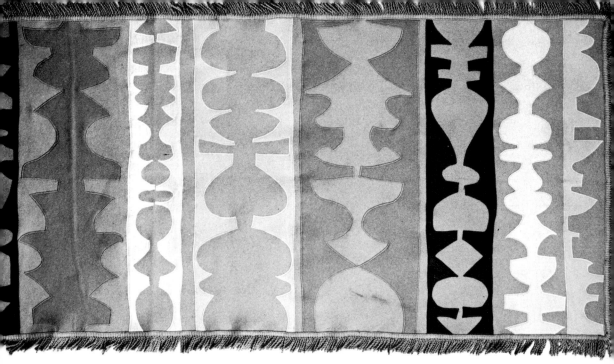

Plate 47. Varying widths of felt are first measured for this appliqué rug. Ornate pedestal shapes are cut from those felt bands and both the positive and negative pieces can be used.

In using a felt background, you are not limited to rectangular or square shapes. An oval or circle will lend itself as well. Fringes and edgings, dyed to match or contrast, can be used to bind or finish the edges of the work. Drapery shops have the widest variety of heavy edgings. Wool fringes are preferable but considerably more expensive than cotton. Tent and awning companies carry a cotton fringe that is quite inexpensive. It comes in many widths and weights, and takes dye nicely. If you are planning to dye your fringe, be sure to buy enough extra to allow for shrinkage.

To hand sew a felt appliqué rug, use a stitch that will hold the edge down firmly. A running stitch, if very tight and near the edge, will do. An overlapping stitch (buttonhole or whip stitch) may be more satisfactory. By hand sewing, you are unlimited in the kinds of shapes you can make, or in the complexity of the shapes. You may add shape on shape for a sculptured effect. There are many directions to go in appliqué rugs. Woolens work beautifully, and tufts, fringes, and layers of felt offer new possibilities. A combination of hand and machine may work well for a rug of simple shapes to which you may wish to add some more ornate pieces.

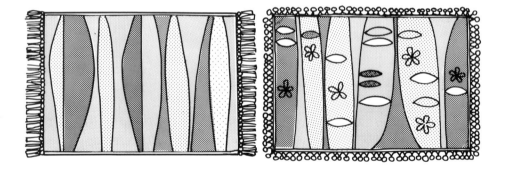

Figure 45. Appliquéd rugs can be made by machine or by hand, but must be well sewn.

Felts and woolens do not soil easily. However, if you are using light colors, it will be helpful to spray the fabric. Several sprays are available which tend to reduce staining and soiling. It is also possible to have fabrics Scotchguarded before using them, if you live in an area where this service is available. Some cleaners do "rain-proofing," which helps on certain fabrics, but this should be checked out with your cleaner before the process is used.

Quilts offer a whole world of possibilities in themselves. One of the most common methods of quilt making, the traditional patch-work, is still the most beautiful. To do a patch-work quilt, blocks are cut and then joined together to make a rectangle large enough to cover a bed. For the appliqué quilt, appliqué designs are added to the blocks. The blocks themselves may be regular in size, with rows of squares or rectangles used, each with its design, as in Figure 46, or they can vary in size so that no two are exactly the same (Figure 47). The appliquéd and patched top must then be finished for use, and this is done by using a second piece of fabric (the same size as the quilt top) for the backing. Between these two layers of fabric goes the padding. Quilting is the process which holds the quilt top, the backing, and the padding together. The process is simply that of a series of stitches which hold the three layers in place.

Cotton batting is the most common padding material, but it requires that the quilting stitches be close together. That is, the rows must be close enough together to hold the batting in place, and to prevent it from matting when washed. If you are appliquéing blocks, you may not wish to have quilting stitches running over your appliqué designs. For me, the best quilting must be designed in terms of the quilt-top pattern. Therefore, if you have appliquéd a series of squares, it may be a more logical

Figure 46. Blocks of the same size are grouped to form bands or patterns across a quilt. While the appliqué design remains the same, colors could vary.

Figure 47. A patch-work approach to a quilt allows for blocks of all shapes and proportions. Often the odd-shaped pieces will suggest objects which will fit them.

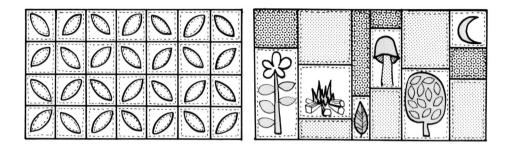

Figure 48. The simple repeat design involves almost no drawing. The quilting here follows the structure of the quilt top.

Figure 49. Appliquéd blocks are alternated with others of printed or plain fabric. The quilting follows the border of each block.

arrangement to let the quilting repeat the design of the squares (see Figure 48). If this means that the rows of quilting stitches are over two or three inches apart, something other than batting should be used. A lightweight cotton blanket works very well. If you prefer a very light coverlet, then a layer of muslin may be enough. Acrilan blankets are excellent for ease of laundering and because the Acrilan has a body or fluffiness which it retains. Batting is also available in Dacron, which, though it is more expensive, is more satisfactory in preventing matting and for washing.

Quilt blocks, because of their size, are easy to handle and a delight to work on. They can be taken with you easily, so that when you have a few minutes to spare you can add a few stitches. A lap robe, crib quilt, or baby quilt is a good beginning project, as it is more limited in size. The appliqué blocks could all be sewn on a single color, or white, and these blocks alternated with patterned or solid colors, as in Figure 49. If the block colors are somewhat limited, more colors can be used in the appliqué. When the blocks are finished, they are joined together with a straight seam. Right sides of the fabrics are placed together, and an edge seam is sewn. This is opened and pressed, and the next block is added.

The quilting itself may be done in any of several ways. If you are working on something small, it can be quilted by laying it out on a table top. The three layers may be placed together, pinned, and sewn, with the quilting always starting at the center and working out. To do a large quilt is a greater undertaking. Commercially made quilt frames are available, as are quilting hoops. These, as well as batting, will usually supply you with quilting directions. The quilting frame serves to keep the fabric layers together and even. A simple quilting frame can be made to suit your needs by using two by two boards and "C" clamps. Purchase the two by twos so that they are four to six inches longer than the quilt measurements. If you were making a quilt four by six feet you would need two boards four feet and six inches long and two boards six feet and six inches long. Staple or tack a muslin fabric around the two longer boards, so that you can later pin into it. Then, let the boards at the two sides (the longer ones) overlap the top and bottom boards and clamp these in the corners as in Figure 50. The quilt backing is then pinned or basted to the muslin-covered boards. The padding or blanket filling is laid on top of this, and then the quilt top goes over all. These three are basted together, starting at the center, going out. Then loosen the "C" clamps, rolling them under from each side, until you have a strip

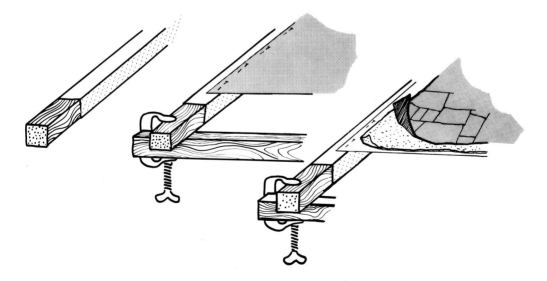

Figure 50. For a homemade quilting frame, muslin is stapled or tacked to the 2 x 2's, which form the sides. C-clamps will hold them together at the corners. The quilt backing is first pinned in place, then the batting or blanket filler, and finally the quilt top.

of quilt about two feet wide, exposed (see Figure 51). This gives you an area small enough to sew on easily. When this area is quilted unroll the sides so that more area is exposed. The frame may be placed over chair backs when in use and can be stored by leaning it up against one wall.

The quilting stitch is simply a running stitch. You may need a stronger needle with a heavier and shorter shaft for the quilting. The quilting can be done using mercerized thread, though there is a thread made especially for quilting which has a slightly heavier and tighter twist. If this is not available, you can use a cotton thread that has been rubbed with beeswax. Always use the thread single strand, not double. The quilting process may be used for the pillows and upholstery pads discussed earlier in this chapter.

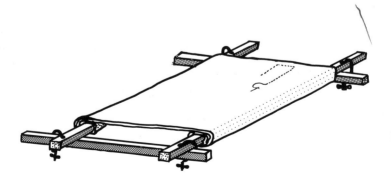

Figure 51. Set up and ready to sew, the side boards are rolled towards the center and under. This makes it easy to reach the center of the quilt. As quilting is finished, it is unrolled and reclamped.

COVERLETS

There are ways of doing coverlets which do not require quilting or quilting frames. You might, for instance, cut and appliqué your quilt blocks leaving a seam allowance. Instead of joining the blocks, sew them, one at a time, onto a single piece of backing fabric. The edges would be turned under and the process would be like that used in the hanging of the "Castle," Color Plate XIII. These could be sewn on in a crazy quilt pattern, using all shapes, or in repeated sizes of squares and rectangles. The backing fabric for this should be heavy enough to hold its shape with the addition of the blocks. A medium weight wool, or fairly tight weave would do. Perhaps a spread no longer in use would provide an available base. Blocks may even be applied to a white bed sheet to make a lightweight summer coverlet. A colored sheet, a sheet blanket of cotton, or a woolen or synthetic blanket would all serve well.

Few projects will give more lasting pleasure than a quilt or coverlet. A collection of a child's favorite toys would make suitable subjects for blocks, as would the flowers of your garden, family pets, or hobbies. Simple geometric shapes can be used effectively with the squares or rectangles being combined with an embroidery stitch.

HEADBOARDS

Doing a headboard requires first that you select a background fabric of the right size and proportion. Once the finished size is determined, allow several inches of extra fabric at each edge. A piece of plywood, cut to the desired size, is then covered with the piece of fabric to be appli-

Figure 52. A headboard design suitable for stitchery. Birds could be cotton appliqué, with the more detailed line work done in embroidery.

Figure 53. A row of garden flowers grow brightly in a headboard appliqué. Fabric can be set into an existing headboard or it can be stretched over a wood panel and hung over the head of the bed.

quéd by folding the fabric around the ply board. This will help determine placement of the design. Remove fabric and appliqué or embroider as desired. When the appliqué design is finished, draw the edges around the board, stapling or tacking them into place. Then frame all with simple molding, and line or finish off the back side.

If you already have a headboard, measure so that a thin plywood piece could be covered and inserted into the existing frame. This can be tacked or nailed into place. It is possible, of course, to use the appliqué panel on a wall, without using a headboard at all. It serves as a headboard without being attached to the bed. Figures 52 and 53 suggest other designs suitable for headboards.

FLAGS AND BANNERS

Much neglected nowadays, flags and banners offer many possibilities. Plate 48 shows a flag I sewed for an old car my husband used to drive. Each side depicted a series of things describing his interests. On this side a heart symbolized his big-hearted nature, and the two seeds were for our two children. The cup suggests his addiction to coffee, and the flowers are a reminder of his green thumb. On the reverse side are a house (for home), a bird (since he is also a pilot), a log (to suggest his enjoyment of the out-of-doors), and books (for his interests in teaching and in art). This kind of flag is possible to have only when one person makes it for another. It is this very personal use of stitchery which makes it such a pleasure to work with.

My son received a flag on his sixth birthday, made by a family friend. On this flag appeared all the things important to a six-year-old boy: trees, baseballs, a bottle of pop, books, food, a million-dollar bill, and (largest of all) his name and age. Flags have been made for teams, for clubs, for camping. Birthday flags, staked out on the yard, help assure that children arriving for a party would find the right house.

Another use for flags is that of announcing your presence. A cabin or summer home might fly a flag to show your return. A back door flag can announce to the neighborhood whether or not it is nap time, and it saves answering numerous little knocks. Flags for house boats and sail boats are always appropriate.

Banners are similar to flags, but are usually suspended from above and can, therefore, be heavier. They can be hung for holidays and special occasions, or to mark a particular site. A series of flower banners were hung at the head and sides of my daughter's bed starting at the ceiling and hanging to the floor. They enclosed the bed in a kind of secret hideaway. These banners were made of percale in three colors; yellow, yellow-green and white. The same colors were used then in the appliqué, and all were hand sewn.

Similar banners were used for my son's room, but on these I depicted his favorite story-book heroes. Roland, Hector, and William the Conqueror lined up around the bed so that all could be seen when he was in bed. On the reverse side, which you saw as you approached the bed, were solid bright colors. These were sewn on a light weight denim, machine stitched.

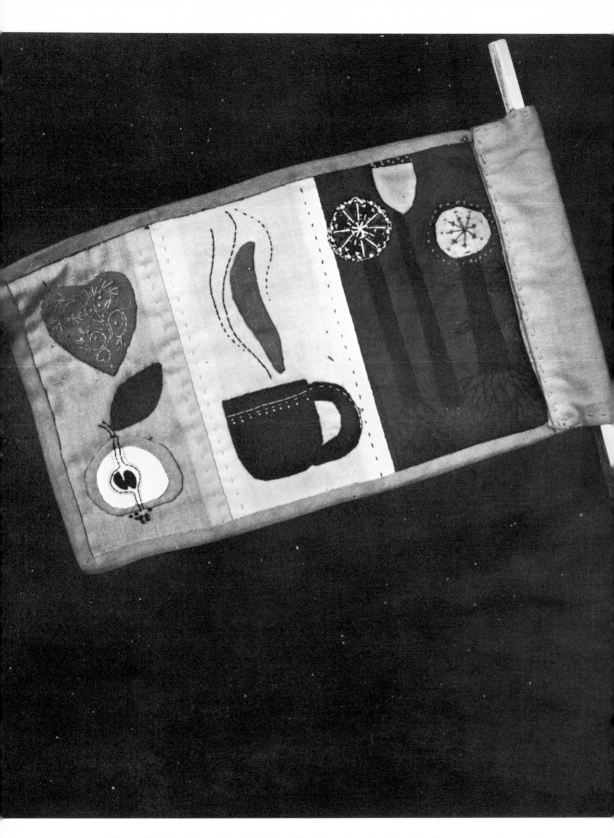

Plate 48. Car Flag. 5 by 9 inches. Hand appliqué and embroidery are used on this two-sided flag, made to be used on a car.

Banners are often made for one-night-stands. If they are to be used just once, on a special occasion, then there are ways of saving time in their construction. Edges need not be hemmed for a single use. A cut or fringed line will do well. Iron-on tape can achieve the effects of detail over larger appliqué areas. Felt will work well, and no hemming or edging is required. The top may be folded over a dowel, and glued or sewn into place. They add festivity to any occasion — garden party or holiday open house.

BOOK COVERS

Appliquéd on cotton or other fine fabric, book covers are simply made. By folding a heavy paper book cover, you can determine how to make one of fabric. It can be done with one long strip, folded at the ends to form envelopes. The book covers slip into these envelopes, as in Figure 54. The appliqué design may reflect the contents of the book, or it may be done with a thought to the owner of the book. It is a pleasure to sew for a book which you treasure yourself, or to sew a book cover as a special gift.

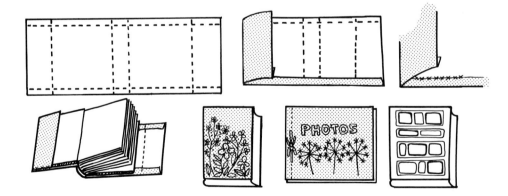

Figure 54. Book covers are a simple and delightful project for stitchery.

TOTE BAGS

Simple construction makes the tote bag a good beginning project, and one well suited for group activity. It is a versatile article suitable for individual use, for school bag, picnic bag, or car carry-all. A rectangle of fabric (fifteen by thirty inches is a good size to start with) is folded in half lengthwise, and sides are joined. Figure 55 describes the step-by-step process. The appliqué can be most easily done while the fabric is still flat, but be sure to measure fold lines. A light stitch to mark the hem allowance will assure that the appliqué design will not run off the edges.

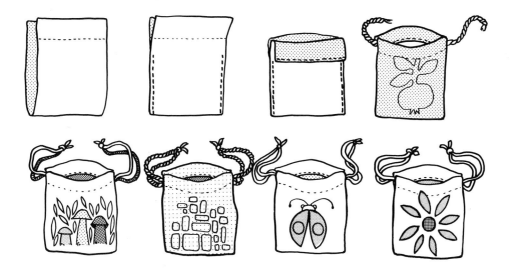

Figure 55. Tote bags are simple to make and allow for a variety of designs.

These provide one of the most obvious uses of stitchery. The directions are simply those of appliqué, provided some allowance has been made at each edge for hemming. A "slot" must be left at top and bottom if the panel is to be hung from a rod. Most fabrics will look and hang better if they are lined, or backed. This can be done before the appliqué work, so that the sewing goes through both layers, or it can be done after the appliqué is complete. Figures 56 and 57 depict both ways. In either case, be sure to allow fabric at top and bottom edges for hanging. A brass rod or wood dowel can be used through the folded edge. Allow about one and one half inches of the rod to extend at each end so that this end can be slipped over a hook. If the hook or rod holder can be hung away from the wall by one or two inches, the fabric has a chance to hang free. I would also use a rod or weight in the lower edge, as this helps to keep the fabric hem even. A long horizontal panel may be too heavy for a rod. Those that stretch out over four feet become more difficult to support. Solid brass begins to bend in the center, and it is not always possible to find a slender curtain rod which is strong enough. A heavy wood dowel will work well, or a two inch by two inch piece of pine around which the top of the panel can be attached.

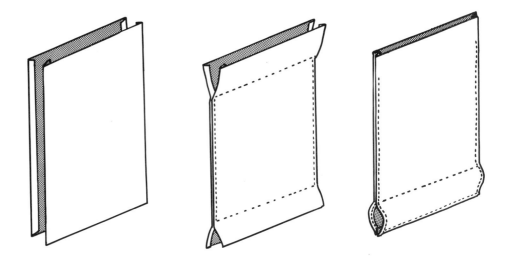

Figure 56. The fabric for a wall hanging can be backed, hemmed, and finished before the appliqué is started.

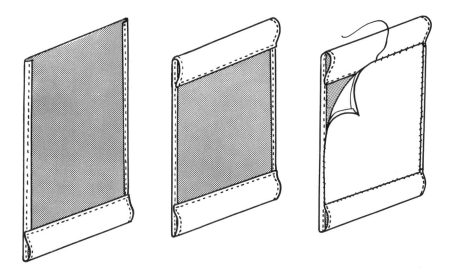

Figure 57. If the appliqué is finished first, then backing and hemming may be done in this manner.

A good project for the beginner as well as the more advanced "stitcher" is found in tablecloths, place mats, or napkins. Tableware seems to invite appliqué. Plate 49 shows a design appliquéd onto ready-made napkins. Fabrics of red, white, and pink were appliquéd on red and white napkins. Each napkin was different, and the designs were drawn from little everyday objects. As the napkins were folded square, the designs pointed into the corners. A single design may be repeated, varying colors from one to the next. The appliqué color of one may provide the background color of another. As well-made napkins are available in a wide range of solid colors, I prefer to purchase them already finished so that my time can be spent on the appliqué. If you prefer, of course, you can make the napkins of linen or cotton, hemming or edging them, and adding your own appliqué designs. A table setting is greatly enriched with even the smallest amount of hand sewing.

A tablecloth design should be done in terms of intended use. The appliqué pattern might appear in the very center, so that it can serve as a centerpiece, or it might be used as a border design. A cloth planned for a buffet service can use appliqué in areas which might otherwise be hidden by plates. Special cloths deserve special treatment, and a holiday seems to invite this treatment. But it might be well to consider a versatile cloth, with napkins or mats that change. A bright red cloth, for example, could be used during the Christmas holidays with green napkins, appliquéd in white and red. In February, the same cloth could be combined with heart or arrow-covered pink and white napkins. For the Fourth of July, a blue napkin with white appliqué stars or stripes would combine with the red cloth for a striking combination. Perhaps you have a tablecloth which you already use, and this will offer a good place to begin. Place mats can be made of almost any fabric, provided it is washable. Designs can be applied in terms of the place setting, so that the appliqué is used as a

Figure 58. Place mats, napkins, and tablecloths are traditional recipients of stitchery, with either appliqué or embroidery being suitable.

Plate 49. The simple forms are easily adapted to appliqué. The running stitch at the edge provides detail and decorative effect.

border at the sides, or in such a way that it relates to dishes that will be used on it. Figure 58 suggests place mat designs suitable for children and adults.

The possible application of stitchery in the home is unlimited. Curtains, draperies and room dividers are just a few more. Children's clothing is an excellent place for your decorative work.

Plate 50. Midnight Flowers. 16 by 17 inches. Cut-through appliqué in browns and black uses five layers of fabric.

CUT-THROUGH WORK

Cut-through work is one of the most intriguing means of appliqué. Though it is more difficult to handle than straight appliqué, it is also more exciting. Color Plates III, V, and XVI show examples of this kind of work, and another can be seen in Plate 50. The cut-through is almost a reverse of appliqué, though the sewing process is similar. Instead of cutting shapes and placing them on a background, a number of background pieces are cut. By cutting into these, and exposing the layers beneath, you get the reverse effect. Designs appear where the fabric is cut away, rather than where fabric is added. Having seen a padded kind of embroidery called Trapunto, as well as the beautifully sewn *molas* of the San Blas Indians, I was inspired to try my own variation of these. To begin, select four or five colors of percale. Other fabrics may be experimented with, but I have found that percale handles best for this more confining work.

Fabric from twelve to fifteen inches square will be an easy size to manage. When the colors are closely related they are easier to work with in the cut-through technique. Because you do not have complete control over where colors will appear within the composition, great contrasts may overwhelm you. In appliqué, you may add an accent color which appears in only one or two spots. But in cut-through, that accent color, (being a layer), would appear each time you cut through to it. To begin then, keep your colors close. After doing one or two, you can recognize what the problems might be, and choose your colors more freely.

Once the fabrics are stacked, a large basting stitch is used to hold them in place, as in Figure 59. This will hold the layers in order until some of your appliqué stitches can hold the fabrics firmly.

Now comes the very exciting part — that of the cutting. A large simple shape is cut out and the fabric removed. Then the edges are sewn down, using a blind or hem stitch. As you sew, always ease the fabric back, away from the cutout section. This will make the applied fabric stand out slightly, and the edge will tend to roll over its stitches. As you sew, a few of the stitches will go through all the layers, holding them together. Not all of the stitches need to go all the way through.

When that shape has been sewn, another may now be cut within that one. This can continue down to the final layer. The pieces which you have cut out and tossed aside can now be used as appliqué over some of the cutout areas. This is the basic procedure for the cut-through, but the possibilities are unlimited. Next, try cutting a series of small shapes from the top fabric. Then, let your scissors reach beneath these to cut one large shape from the second layer of fabric. The underneath layer must, of course, be sewn first. After sewing a few pieces you will become adept at

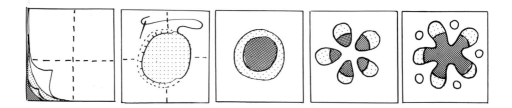

Figure 59. Cut-through stitchery is accomplished by stacking several layers of fabrics. They are then cut into to reveal the colors beneath.

reaching through these cut strips so that you can sew the underneath layer.

Once you have mastered these two basic procedures (shapes cut within shapes, and shapes overlapping other cutouts), you are ready to go ahead. After that, it is a matter of working, and as you do you will find new ways of approaching your designs. Variations of these two make almost all shapes possible.

A very small detail in the cutout will be the most difficult to sew. If you want small dots, or circles, I suggest that these be appliquéd on rather than cut through, as in Plate 50. Sometimes a shape can be cut out, and then sewn right back into the same spot. The turned under hem of both edges will leave a space showing between the shapes.

At times you may wish to cut through the top layer and want to go directly to the third, rather than use the color of the second layer. This is possible if you will first cut your top shape out. Then, reaching through that opening with your scissors blades, cut the second layer back further than the top opening. That will reveal the third layer.

Embroidery can be combined most effectively with the cut-through. Color Plate XV shows this use, as does Plate 34. Because of the layers and the cutting, your finished piece of cut-through work will probably not be perfectly square. Mine never are. Therefore, these are finished in a different way. Trim the edges until they are more nearly straight. Then cut a bias binding of the same fabric, about one and one-half inches wide, to be sewn around all four edges, as in Figure 60. Some of that same binding can then be used to make loops for hanging the panel. Another solution for hanging may be the addition of a strip of fabric along the top edge on the back side, through which a rod can be slipped. Either way works satisfactorily.

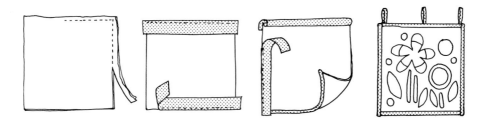

Figure 60. The completed piece of cut-through can be bound and finished with a bias strip.

The cut-through is difficult to handle in very large pieces, and seems most suitable for small hangings or for pillows. The same technique may be used in small areas on panels for regular appliqué. That is, a shape can be applied to the background fabric, then cut through. While it is more difficult, the cut-through seems to me to be the most challenging of all appliqué forms.

PROJECTS SUITABLE FOR CHILDREN

Most children enjoy the bright colors and varied textures of yarns, threads, and fabrics. These are the familiar materials of every day. They are further intrigued by the use of scissors and needles, and are, therefore, receptive to the use of stitchery as another art form. If the materials of stitchery could be provided in class rooms or homes alongside the paints, papers, and crayons, we would see a delightful increase in this activity. It should be offered as another medium, another direction. Some children prefer paint, some crayons, and others water color. Still others will prefer fabric, and the choice should be available.

It would be necessary to give some basic instruction. The proper use of scissors and how to thread a needle are skills which must be mastered. A basic running stitch will serve in the beginning.

Stitchery can easily be introduced through other projects. For example, a class working with puppets might use appliqué for puppet costumes. A stage curtain or back drop might be done with stitchery, with fabric appliqué suggesting the forest, castles, or mountains appropriate to the play.

A mural representing an area of study can be completed in stitchery as well as with paints or papers. These materials will bring forth new ideas and new uses for yarns and scraps. All children can work on one large panel — or each member can contribute a portion or block to a larger piece.

Nature study might provide a means for this individual work, with each child contributing a small appliquéd panel depicting one flower or animal of that locale. Combined, they would present a marvelous composite of what was native to the area. The same approach could be used with leaves, insects, fruits, birds, buildings, or tools. This kind of project is suitable for any group, whether classroom, club, neighborhood, or scouts.

Groups can also work on individual projects with a similarity in terms of theme or use. It is helpful in group projects if the basic structure remains the same, letting individual ideas come through in color and fabric choice, and design. Most of those projects listed earlier can be adapted for children's projects. They can manage pillows, tote bags, place mats, or panels. A few further group projects are listed here, starting with more simple ones. For a child, using needle and thread can be like drawing. Cut fabric is like cut paper. If they have the materials, even children of three can produce delightfully imaginative stitchery.

SIGNAL FLAGS

Using a rectangle of fabric, hem three edges by turning the fabric under (or fringe the edges if you prefer). The fourth edge can be glued over a dowel. The appliqué shapes are then cut in terms of signal designs, symbols, weather warnings, or forecasts. Use a simple running stitch for appliqué. Troops or clubs will enjoy designing their own signals.

TENT FLAGS

A troop or patrol may wish to identify its own tent with a flag. Or a back yard pup-tent or tree-fort might "need" to fly its colors. Fabric is cut and hemmed as the signal flag. Perhaps an acorn (if camped near an oak), a spider, or a camp fire will be a suitable subject. Some particular interest or experience may suggest a theme.

STORAGE BAGS

This bag has rigid sides and bottom for carrying or storage. It is more difficult to sew than a tote bag, but offers some protection to contents. Use a five-gallon ice cream container or similar cylindrical container or box. Place carton on fabric (heavy cotton, denim, twill, etc.) and draw around it, allowing an extra two inches all around. Turn upside down and glue fabric to bottom surface. The two-inch allowance is clipped and glued to the sides of the box. Wrap fabric around the box to determine size needed and join with one side seam. Allow extra fabric at the top for more carrying space and for a fold-over for draw string or rope-tie.

THE POTENTIALS OF STITCHERY

There are many appropriate ways of using stitchery of large scale in architectural installations and interiors other than homes. The "Foods and Wines" panel, Color Plate X, was one of a series done for a coffee shop. Another is shown in Plate 51. These were stretched over plywood, framed at the sides with two by four inch redwood, and well mounted. Other panels for restaurants have been hung, banner-like, from wood drapery rods. "Thicket," Plate VII, hangs from a two by two over which the top edge is folded. One of the best methods is that of attaching a large panel to a two by two inch or a two by four inch board, and then attaching that board to a wall. Factors which should be considered in doing large installations are fire-proofing of fabric, and treatment to make it moth-proof and moisture-resistant. Many upholstery fabrics now come already treated in this way. For commercial installations I most often work with a machine appliqué panel, with hand-sewn details. On pieces not too large in scale (a maximum of four to six feet in any direction) I find stretching and framing to be most satisfactory. Everyone feels a need to touch stitchery, because of the very inviting texture. And a panel, stretched over wood, seems to hold up better than a free hanging fabric when it is handled or touched frequently.

There are few limits to the uses of stitchery. It can be the home art of all homemakers, and one which falls within the range and ability of nearly everyone. But it is not limited to practical application in crafts or to a decorative use. Its potential as a serious art form is being explored more and more by artists everywhere. However, it has only begun — there is so much to be learned, enjoyed, explored, and produced.

The development of individual and personal work in stitchery is as essential for the teacher as for the person completely new to the medium. Anyone can learn the skills — but satisfying, meaningful work grows when the ideas come through personal experience, when the approach is open to new forms of expression, and when the "stitcher" develops an awareness of design, color, and pattern.

Plate 52. Seed Structure. 18 by 22 inches.